D0200403

INNER REVOLUTION

ALSO BY ROBERT THURMAN

*Tsong Khapa's Speech of Gold: Reason and
Enlightenment in the Central Philosophy of Tibet*

The Tibetan Book of the Dead

Essential Tibetan Buddhism

INNER
REVOLUTION

::::

Life, Liberty, and the

Pursuit of Real Happiness

ROBERT THURMAN

RIVERHEAD BOOKS

A MEMBER OF PENGUIN PUTNAM INC.

NEW YORK

1998

Riverhead Books
a member of
Penguin Putnam Inc.
200 Madison Avenue
New York, NY 10016

Library of Congress Cataloging-in-Publication Data

Thurman, Robert A. F.
Inner revolution: life, liberty, and the pursuit of real happiness /
by Robert Thurman.
p.   cm.
ISBN 1-57322-090-6
1. Buddhism—China—Tibet.   2. Buddhism—Doctrines.
3. Spiritual life—Buddhism.   I. Title.
BQ7604.T498   1998   97-44086   CIP
294.3'420423—dc21

Printed in the United States of America

1   3   5   7   9   10   8   6   4   2

This book is printed on acid-free paper. ♾

Book design by Chris Welch

To Shakyamuni the Buddha,
Founder of the inner revolution in our world,
In deepest gratitude and ever-growing admiration.

Your champion insight into selflessness,
Inexhaustible love for beings,
Powerful comprehension of the minute processes
Of history as theater of human evolution,
And inconceivable competence in freeing beings—
All moved You to teach deep relativity
And begin the cool, inexorable, inner revolution;
Founding the Jewel Community for love of freedom,
Introducing generosity, justice, and tolerance,
Enterprise, concentration, and creative genius
To truly civilize our planet home of living beings
In Your Buddhaverse You called "Tolerable"!

And at our postmodern end of history,
to His Holiness the Fourteenth Dalai Lama,
Prince of Peace and Philosopher King of Tibet,
In amazed appreciation of Your creative effort.

For the people of Tibet and of the whole world—
Champion of the teaching, deep, vast, and exquisite,
Simple Shakya monk, Shakyamuni's devoted heir,
Upholder of the common human religion of kindness,
Explorer of the sciences of mind, spirit, society, and nature—
You exemplify the fine intelligence and the good heart,

You bring hope and boundless positivity when all seems
    doomed,
You make peace the path as well as thus the realistic goal,
You live again and again to continue inner revolution,
Effectual for all beings, believers or nonbelievers,
From all world religions and all world sciences,
Blessing other species and all of nature!

Acknowledgments

I have been working on this book since my address "The Politics of Enlightenment" to the Lindisfarne Association in 1976, so the list of those to whom I am indebted is a long one.

In the process of writing, I have had the instruction of many people. To thank those whose teachings and writings have been crucially helpful: Vimalakirti, Nagarjuna, Asanga, Shantideva, Tsong Khapa, the Great Fifth Dalai Lama, Plato, Thomas Paine, Thomas Jefferson, Max Weber, Buckminster Fuller, Peter Berger, Philip Slater, Riane Eisler, Ken Wilber, Jeremy Rifkin, William Greider. To thank those who have personally inspired me on this topic: David Wills and David Little, who helped me learn so much from the inimitable Max Weber; Peter Berger, who helped me with his challenging inquiry; David Spangler, who helped me see the positive potential in the future; Tara Tulku Rinpoche, who made old doctrines new and creative; my friends Joel McCleary and Toinette Lippe, who helped me think about effective action and practical compassion; and, most important, my wife, Nena, my continuing teacher, my eldest son, Ganden, who helped me put this book together. I must also thank the many students who have attended my classes and lectures on this and related topics over the past twenty-five years—the great privilege and joy of teaching is to see new things about what you thought you knew when you reinvestigate them in the light of others' need to know.

For their indispensable help in getting this book written in its final form, I must thank my agent, Lynn Nesbit, for keeping things moving during the ups and downs of the process, her keen eyes always clear on target. I sincerely thank my consulting editor, Jisho Cary Warner, who has ably helped me with several previous books as well, for all her thoughtful help and hard work. Most important, from the beginning of this project, my special thanks to my good friend and long-term editor, Amy Hertz, for her faith, patience, persistence, critical and creative intellect, and strenuous effort. I also thank everyone at Riverhead Books, especially Susan Petersen, the publisher, and Jennifer Repo, editorial assistant.

Finally, first and last, I have to thank Shakyamuni the Buddha and His Holiness the Dalai Lama, without whom I would have nothing to write about; the Venerable Geshe Wangyal, without whom I would not have been able to write anything;

and again, my beloved soul mate, Nena, without whom I would not have wanted to write anything; and all my beloved five children, Taya, Ganden, Uma, Dechen, Mipam, and three grandchildren, without whom I would not have such a clear sense of whom to write this for.

Robert A. F. Thurman
Gandendechenay, Woodstock, New York
November 1997

Contents

FOREWORD

*B*ob Thurman is one of my oldest Western friends. He has been thinking about this *Inner Revolution* for a long time. I remember we had talked about it in Dharamsala years ago.

For Tibetan Buddhists, these ideas are not revolutionary; naturally, when you transform your individual mind, the whole society is transformed. As Buddhists we believe that the Buddha had the compassionate plan to help all sentient beings, as well as the wisdom to understand how it works.

Thurman explained to me how some Western thinkers have assumed that Buddhism has no intention to change society, since the Buddha left his throne and created monasteries, and renunciation is fundamental in the Buddhist path. Thurman's book provides a timely corrective to any lingering notions about Buddhism as an uncaring religion.

I think Thurman gives new insights into the Tibetan society and its special Buddhist culture. Thurman pointed out to me the essential difference between the highly militaristic European, Russian, and Chinese feudal societies and our peaceful, monastic, happy—though not materially developed—traditional Tibetan lifestyle. Thurman is keen to challenge the modern notion that material progress is the ultimate good.

I have noticed that Westerners tend to become cynical about politics and lose hope that any political leader will ever do anything useful or even intelligent. Perhaps reading about the history of some of the leaders of Buddhist societies, such as the Indian kings Ashoka and Udayi and my predecessor the Fifth Dalai Lama, may encourage people that politics can be a Buddhist practice too, and that benevolent and skillful social action can be a path toward enlightenment. It is important that we do not become discouraged and that we shoulder our responsibility for this world and its future generations with great determination and foresight. Thurman's book attempts to present this aspect of the Buddhist concept of serving others. I commend him for his careful study and clear explanations, and I recommend his insights for your own reflections.

October 8, 1997

PREFACE

I was born in the summer of 1941, and my first memories of the world beyond my family have World War II as the backdrop. We crossed over from Manhattan and went down to the Brooklyn Navy Yard to see off my uncle Byng. He set sail in late 1944 on his tanker ship, a proud captain finally getting away from his shipbuilding duties to see some action. I felt left behind as this man I hardly knew patted me on the head, walked up the ramp onto his ship, and went away. I remember afterward a collage of incidents reflecting the anguish of my mother's parents, who lived with us, when Byng's ship blew up in the English Channel, torpedoed by an uninformed submarine the day after Germany surrendered. He was carrying a cargo of aviation gasoline, and no survivors or remains ever were found. Purse and Dunie, as my grandparents called each other, departed in disbelief for coastal England and France, looking in camps and hospitals,

1

hoping desperately to find an amnesiac but living Byng. They continued their search for several years after the war amid the confusion of displaced persons. Dunie had a stroke and subsequently lost her mind, and Purse eventually gave up. Byng's was an innocent death, preventable but for a trigger-happy hand behind a powerful weapon.

During my teens in the fifties, I remember air-raid drills, the sirens on top of a pole at the corner of Eighty-first and Lexington going off at regular intervals. We were told that there was a danger of atomic war with the Russians and that New York City might be a target. I remember the joy of celebrating my birthday being clouded by images of Hiroshima and Nagasaki. At my Anglophile private school, I pursued my studies of French and Latin, algebra and English history, Shakespeare, Homer, and the Bible. I skated along on a surface of bright-eyed, bushy-tailed enthusiasm for life and Western culture that bubbled above the dark currents in which lurked the sudden end of the world in nuclear holocaust. Finally the ice cracked and I could do nothing but face the existential crisis the world had brought itself to. I needed answers to both the world's danger and my own fear of the potential for devastating violence.

I questioned everything said by everyone after that realization, except the one continuous report to myself that I was "me." I questioned who I was and why I held the opinions I held, feeling an urgent need to pin down my identity, but I never wondered if I *was* at all. I wanted to get to know myself, whatever happened to the world. I encountered my own mortality when I lost one eye in an accident, and remained focused on myself. I went on vision quests; I traveled as a pilgrim all the way to India, pursuing myself, giving up everything to get to the land of holy gurus; I suffered my father's death and became ever more determined to find myself. Briefly back in New York for the funeral, I met Geshe Wangyal, a Mongolian monk living just down the road in New Jersey.

I felt a power, an intensity around him in his pink house with its crude and colorful chapel; on his small acre next to a concrete Russian Orthodox church. In his presence it was hard for me to speak; my knees felt weak and my stomach unsettled. Yet the amazing thing was that Geshe Wangyal himself seemed as if he were not there. He had nothing to do with me, to me, or for me. He seemed fully content and unconcerned for himself. When I couldn't find "him," I was forced to ask myself, *Who is this "me" I've been pursuing?* At twenty-one years old, after dropping out of college, leaving a new marriage, barely able to take care of myself, I felt a hint of something beyond my self.

Geshe Wangyal was unlike anyone I had ever met. As a teenaged monk he had nearly died of typhoid in the hot Black Sea summer. His mother heard that the monks had given him up for dead, so she came to the monastery and spent three days sucking the pus and phlegm out of his throat and lungs to keep him from suffocating. When he awoke, the first thing he was told was that she had succumbed to the disease she saved him from and died on the very day he recovered. He was appalled when he observed that though he felt grief at the news, another current in his mind would not let him think of anything else except his overwhelming thirst after his ten-day fever. Noting this dreadful degree of selfishness, he resolved then and there to give his last ounce of effort to freeing himself and others from such involuntarily selfish impulses. I had never encountered directly such unconditional compassion in my entire life. I was hooked.

Geshe Wangyal told me he wouldn't be my guru, since he felt he was no high being and that I was not capable of traveling the difficult path of spiritual development. But he conceded that whatever he had learned of value in his life had come from Tibetan books, and he had an inkling that I might find something of value in them myself. Since I was not a monk, I couldn't stay in his monastery, so I would have to find my own lodging. He agreed to feed me and to teach me to read Tibetan if I taught English to some young monks he had in his care. One week later I was back in New Jersey, cleaned up, and ready for studies, having sold my ticket to New Delhi to pay the rent.

During the first Tibetan lesson, Greshe Wangyal spoke of suffering, and my world shifted dramatically. We're born, we get sick, we get old, we die. We crave comfort and happiness but never seem to find it. We fear losing what little we have. It was a mind-opening experience for me to learn that living without knowing what I was doing and why I was doing it was causing me to suffer. Living with the fear of the world blowing up; chasing after knowledge, sex, pleasure, and myself; and trying to escape reality certainly left me coming up empty—all I did was crave more of everything. Before this lesson, the answers to my questions seemed to be just around the corner. I'd turn the corner only to find something else to desire, and the chase would start all over again. It was the chase that was making me miserable, and somewhere inside me was an idea that was driving the chase. For the first time, someone was telling me that there was a way to free myself from the whole chase. I was being asked to *face* suffering, but at the same time, I was discovering that there was a way to *end* that suffering.

Preoccupation with myself was the core problem, the center of the malfunction in my mechanism that prevented me from enjoying life as much as I felt I could, from being as good to others as I wanted to be, from understanding all I wanted to. I began to see meaning in reorienting my life toward freeing myself from "me."

From 1962 until 1966, I lived on almost nothing, maybe a hundred dollars a month; I wore jeans and T-shirts for the first two years, and then, after being ordained, the simple Buddhist monk's robe—threefold in the Tibetan tradition, including a maroon skirt, a maroon upper shawl, and a yellow overshawl for special occasions. I didn't spend a dollar on consumer goods, rarely watched television, listened to no music, read only Dharma books belonging to monasteries, and meditated a lot. No longer did I worry about cars and motorcycles, suits and good-looking shoes. I shaved my head periodically. I never traveled unless someone requested me to do so and paid for it. I was a vegetarian for several of those years as well.

When I look back at my experience during this time, I feel as if I existed in a state of orgasm that was diffused throughout my body and throughout my day, rather than concentrated in the genitals and focused on fleeting moments of intense excitation. I had a great sense of inner well-being, for a change, after having been a teenaged love-seeker and then a married man, never getting enough in either case.

I did not concern myself with money, family, future, career, or competition in any area of life. I had less than ever, yet I was far more content. All I wanted was to stay in the 2,500-year-old Buddhist community of seekers of enlightenment, to be embraced as a monk. My inner world was rich, full of insights and delightful visions, with a sense of luck and privilege at having access to such great teachers and teachings and the time to study and try to realize them. Such longing as I still felt was directed at inner states that I imagined lay farther up the path toward enlightenment.

I wanted nothing more than to follow Geshe-la's example. He, however, insisted it would be better for me to continue study and meditation without becoming a formally ordained monk. I was persistent, and he finally agreed to take me with him to India, to introduce me to monastic teachers there.

In 1964, Geshe Wangyal introduced me formally to His Holiness the Dalai Lama at Sarnath, India, the site where Buddha first taught about suffering. He described me as a crazy American boy, very intelligent and with a good heart (though a little proud), who spoke Tibetan well and had learned something about Buddhism. I wanted to be a monk—I would become the first Westerner to be ordained in that tradition—and Geshe Wangyal was leaving it up to His Holiness to decide. He would leave me in India with the Tibetan refugee community, under His Holiness's charge, to study more about Buddhism. His Holiness looked at me curiously and asked Geshe Wangyal to bring me up to Dharamsala for another audience. He would personally arrange for my studies.

In Dharamsala, the seat of the Tibetan exile community, His Holiness met with me frequently to check my progress, but he was not to be my main teacher. A place was arranged for me to stay with Dagyab Rinpoche, one of the highest lamas of old Tibet. He was then only a year older than I but, like most lamas, had been trained to teach since he was a small child. Khen Losang Dondrub, the abbot of His Holiness's personal monastery, Namgyal College, was assigned to teach me Buddhist philosophy. His Holiness's own senior tutor, His Eminence Ling Rinpoche, was to be my moral preceptor concerning my wish to be a monk. Rounding out my education was Tibetan medicine, astronomy, and astrology, topics I had not thought I'd need to study on my way to becoming a monk.

I had a fascinating year in Dharamsala, studying and meditating all the time, learning about the Tibetan universe. My meetings with His Holiness soon became weekly occurrences. During these conversations he quickly reviewed my progress and deflected my questions to my more senior teachers. Then he turned to topics in Western culture that interested him, which were numerous. He asked me about Freud, Plato, Jefferson, the United States Constitution, democracy, automobiles, airplanes, and nuclear physics. It was difficult for me to describe these things in Tibetan, and often I had to use English words or coin new Tibetan words as I went along. I thought about liberty and freedom in the context of American society. Liberty to do what? Pursue happiness? Were we really happy? Were we really free?

Finally His Holiness and Ling Rinpoche did give permission for me to be formally ordained as a monk. Ling Rinpoche gave me the preliminary renunciation vows, and His Holiness administered the final ceremony of acceptance of the 252 precepts a month or so later. Ling Rinpoche impressed upon me the solemn responsibility I had as the first Westerner to receive this ordination in the Tibetan tradition of Buddhist monasticism. I was honored, and overwhelmed.

In the Christian West and the Buddhist Far East, monks and nuns enter a life of penance and mortification, dressed in their black, gray, or dark-brown habits. By contrast, the Indian and Tibetan monastic movements are based on Buddha's discovery of the middle way between hedonism and asceticism and are focused on withdrawing from unimportant pleasures in order to engage in the evolution toward ultimate pleasure—freedom from the prison of the self that pursues suffering. The Tibetan culture had in place a structure of total support for my dedication to the study, practice, and performance of the teachings. I plunged into the community of Tibetans in India who had fled the massacre wrought by the communist Chinese, not realizing then what a unique culture it was for its ability to encourage me.

I discovered in India how little it takes to live comfortably once one changes priorities. The absence of electricity made every evening a candlelight celebration, encouraged me to sleep early and get up with the sun to use the clear daylight and fresh mind of morning. Lack of running water gave me the opportunity to participate in the invigorating exercise of carrying buckets of water from a spring, enjoying the fellowship of my neighbors as I performed this daily task. Lack of telephones enabled me to concentrate on the person in front of me without interruption. This is what my life was like, living in a Tibetan refugee camp. It was a daily illumination.

After more than a year, I had the sense that I had accomplished my mission in Dharamsala, and I began to feel restless in the tiny Himalayan town. I wanted to return to America, to see friends, try out my new lifestyle at home, even though as a monk, my vows, not to mention my robes, might make me a little conspicuous. I felt the monastic discipline could help me adopt a freer lifestyle in the middle of a world that once had brought me so much dissatisfaction, could make me more at ease because I wouldn't have the pressure of seeking a mate, a job, or any possessions.

The goal in Tibetan Buddhism is that as each individual conquers delusions like hatred, it becomes possible for her or him to help the whole world do it. Freeing other beings from their suffering, I was taught, should be the goal of one's own meditative practice. Naive and idealistic, I nevertheless held in my mind that I was setting an example about the inner life: to find freedom first for oneself and then for the larger society. It didn't work out as well as I had expected.

While I was trying to manifest my ideals, my contemporaries were having terrible identity crises and getting lost in drugs. I had felt sane and happy enough in my monastic retreat, but now I was frustrated that I could not share with anyone else the relief I felt. The Buddhist monk's outfit had been invented by the Buddha so that people would respect a seeker of enlightenment, but I noticed that although they might have respected a great personage like the Dalai Lama, no one in America really respected an American monk at that time. No one among my friends or family could understand why I was wearing a red robe and wandering around with my head shaved.

By the mid-sixties, the Vietnam War was heating up and

I was haunted by the image of Tri Quang Duc, a spry old Vietnamese monk who sometime in 1965 made a decision that would impact millions of people's lives. Smiling cheerfully at some video camerapersons, he calmly approached a chosen site, sat down in meditation posture, doused himself with gasoline, and was suffused with roaring flames. He did not recoil in either pain or terror, and all the while a slight smile spread across his lips. After fully fifty seconds of blackening, sizzling, charring consumption by the flames, his body lost structural integrity and imploded. He had remained unmoved from the peace he knew.

At least, this is how I remember that famous film clip. It was not just the horror of seeing a human being burned alive: it was the evident truth of his ability to burn yet remain unconcerned with the burning; it was the eerie power of seeing him choose immolation in order to bring to their senses those who were so driven by their passions they were frying children with napalm and annihilating hundreds of thousands of adults.

Most everyone I knew was unimpressed. They thought he was either mad or drugged, but I couldn't shake the vision of it. His steps in that film were sure, not wobbly. He was an old man, and death couldn't have been far. He seemed long past fearing it; he understood it and was able to face it. Tri Quang Duc showed his true conquest of anger. He let the flames of hatred consume his body without letting his happiness be disturbed.

Isolated in the middle of all these forces, I felt like a stranger in a strange land—not skillful enough to manifest my dream of bringing happiness to those around me; not wanting to return to my old way of life. There seemed no future for me in America as a monk, no community to support my progress like there had been among the Tibetans, and no way to share with my contemporaries the joy and clarity I had found.

So, after much soul-searching, I left the monkhood. Though I knew I had made the right decision, I still felt a great sense of shame knowing that my teachers, particularly Ling Rinpoche and the Dalai Lama, would feel deeply disappointed. Geshe Wangyal had never recommended my becoming a monk—now that I was one, he would not take responsibility for my reconsideration. I resigned my vows and tried to give my robes back to him, but he referred me to His Holiness. I resolved to make up for my failing by pursuing my practice as ardently as I did as a monk, but at the same time I felt too proud to return to my previous life in lay society. I was caught in the mistake of confusing a modicum of knowledge and a few intense meditative experiences with genuine, stable, nonregressing, enlightened awareness. The question was what to do with myself. While I respected my lamas in India and my teacher in New Jersey, I felt I had nothing to learn from anyone else in the West. Obviously, I had a long way to go.

My greatest danger at this time was the temptation to

become a guru. People knew I had been a Buddhist monk, and it was hard for them to distinguish between a monk and an ex-monk. I knew enough of the main teaching systems of Tibetan Buddhism and could meditate well enough to achieve altered perceptions and insights into the nature of mind to have built up a following. Though I was still proud, I did have the example of Geshe Wangyal, who had always refused to gather a big circle of disciples. If he, learned as he was, wouldn't become a guru, how could I presume to be a spiritual master? It was obvious that I would have to find some sort of profession to earn my living independently so I would never be tempted to use people's desire for spiritual growth for my own economic gain. I decided that I wanted to learn more Buddhist languages, read more Buddhist texts, and continue to discover the vast new continent of the Dharma. The only lay institution in America comparable to monasticism is the university, so in the end I turned to academia.

Luckily, I found a soul mate, Nena, with whom I fell in love, and began to rediscover family, school, profession, and even America. She also became my teacher, my "show-me" spiritual friend, who was less interested in high-flown talk or abstruse practices than in daily performance of the teaching in positive action. We soon experienced the miracle of the birth of a delightful boy, named Ganden by Geshe Wangyal after the joyous paradise of Maitreya the future Buddha. He was soon joined by his sister, who naturally owned the name of the Indian Mother-goddess, Uma. More beautiful children followed.

I found it hard to integrate my Buddhist way of life with the world of modern America and the competitive demands of professional academia. Having a role to play—that of an impoverished young graduate student with a new family—at least provided some cushion. After I finished three years of grueling study of languages, social sciences, Asian history, and world philosophy while trying to learn to be a husband to Nena and a father to two energetic new babies, I got a research grant to visit India. I would be able to see my teachers again. It was 1970, and I had not been there for five years.

I was apprehensive about how the Dalai Lama would behave toward me in the wake of my resigning the monkhood, and I was tense at our first meeting. I approached, bowed clumsily, and before I could make proper introductions, my three-year-old son, Ganden, jumped into the Dalai Lama's lap, hugged him, and knocked the glasses right off his face. The Dalai Lama burst out laughing—the ice was broken, and we returned to the enthusiastic friendship we had shared five years before. At the end of our long discussion, His Holiness gave me recommendations about whom I should study with for my dissertation, how he could help me himself (the book I was translating was one of his favorites), where we should live, and so on. Then he took my hands and Nena's together in his, and he gave us his blessing.

When I completed my degree several years later and
began to teach, I was appalled to discover in the Western literature and in my colleagues' minds a massive and systematic distortion of Eastern civilizations in general, and
Buddhist civilization in particular. This misinformation came
from the European "authorities" Weber, Freud, Marx, and
Durkheim and was perpetuated by contemporary writers,
even by translators. The basic prejudices I encountered were
that Asians have no individualism; that they do not distinguish themselves perceptually, much less intellectually, as
individuals; and that they basically believe life is cheap.
Therefore they have little interest in ethical systems and give
themselves over to "Oriental despotism" without blinking
an eye. Among these "Asians," the Buddhists are the most
extreme, teaching the annihilation of self and life as the highest good, being "socially apathetic," "other-worldly," "mystical," "world-rejectors" (Weber's phrases). Though these
prejudices are utterly absurd to anyone who has ever lived
within an Asian culture, I found that they were entrenched
in my colleagues' minds and spread routinely to students, in-
fecting the entire body of Western culture. I had seen firsthand just the opposite behaviors exhibited by a people in
exile. I had watched my own teachers work tirelessly for the
sake of others. I had experienced the support of an alien
community in my endeavor as a monk. I had seen—through
modern vestiges of that ancient way of life—a movement
that began 2,500 years ago with the enlightenment of the

Buddha to create a pure world of which the foundation is helping each individual transform into his or her full potential. That full potential is nothing less than becoming a totally enlightened being, a buddha just as great as the historical figure. Never has there been, before or since the Buddha's teachings, a more positive philosophy nor one that cherishes the individual quite so much. I had to set the record straight.

My battle went on against a backdrop of being a young professor struggling to get tenure—a drawn-out campaign that is enough to ruin the psychic integrity, family life, and personal health of anyone. You have six years in a profession that is underpaid during which you must illuminate hundreds of students; please all your colleagues around the country with your brilliance, moral fiber, charm, and service to the profession; make your mark on your community with special events; publish at least two books, half a dozen articles, and a number of reviews in leading journals; and generally become indispensable to your school. You must be careful not to be too popular with the students, not to outshine your colleagues too much, and not to be too controversial in your scholarship. If you do not get tenure in your sixth year, though you may move and in another couple of years get it at a less prestigious institution (usually somewhere far away from where you and your family have made your home), more than likely you never will get it anywhere and will have to go back to some sort of professional school and retool for another career.

Whatever the source of the miracle, in December of 1978 I was granted tenure, the first Buddhist in the history of the Amherst College Religion department to be so honored.

My commitment to helping others end their suffering only intensified, and I very much wanted to expose people to the great teachers I had met in India so that they could experience firsthand what it's like to be in the presence of someone dedicated to your happiness.

His Holiness has always been dignified and magnetically charming. During the seventies, he performed many formal retreats, mastering the various rituals of tantra, a precious form of Buddhism protected and preserved by the Tibetans after it was nearly wiped out of India more than 1,000 years ago. In this tradition, the individual literally reinvents the world as a place inhabited by enlightened beings in an enlightened environment. This, I believe, is the source of the charisma most people feel around him now.

Through most of the seventies, the Dalai Lama was blocked from teaching the world because of an agreement between the Nixon administration and the Chinese Communists. During the Carter administration, it finally became possible for him to visit America.

Amherst College, as well as Harvard University, where I moonlighted as a visiting professor, became the first schools to host His Holiness during that visit in September of 1979.

When I greeted him in America that fall, we had not seen each other for eight years. He was the same cheerful, lively person I had known. But there was something new and awesome about him. The night before he landed in New York, I dreamed he was manifesting the pure land mandala palace of the Kalachakra Buddha right on top of the Waldorf Astoria building. The entire collection of dignitaries of the city, mayors and senators, corporate presidents and kings, sheikhs and sultans, celebrities and stars—all of them were swept up into the dance of 722 deities of the three buildings of the diamond palace like pinstriped bees swarming on a giant honeycomb. The amazing thing about the Dalai Lama's flood of power and beauty was that it appeared totally effortless. I could feel the space of His Holiness's heart, whence all this arose. It was relaxed, cool, an amazing well of infinity.

I returned to India with His Holiness and my family for a year-long sabbatical in 1979. During this time, he opened my eyes to the tragedy and preciousness of Tibet itself. It is a nation of six million souls, an occupied country of one million square miles at an average altitude of fifteen thousand feet. Tibet can seem to be a lost cause, a remote Himalayan fastness overrun by the most populous nation on earth—a nation bent on destroying a precious culture and a special people with a rich tradition for helping us deal with the difficulties we face in the late twentieth century. I had lived with Tibetan refugees in the sixties in the early years of their diaspora, shared tin houses with them in Dharamsala. I thought the tide of Chinese expansion was irreversible, and I had brashly advised His Holiness to abandon his political responsibility, to give up his kingdom, and to present himself as a world leader of Dharma. With superhuman patience, he said he admired the idea but could not follow it in the real world, since his people depended on him too much. Tibet was his responsibility.

I remembered my dream of the Dalai Lama manifesting a pure, protected land even in the middle of New York City, and I realized that it was indeed possible for Tibet to become free once more. Not only possible, but necessary and inevitable. Size cannot make China right. Little Tibet has the power of truth on its side.

In 1987, Nena and I went to Tibet proper for the first time. What a revelation! It was a shattering experience for us to meet the Tibetans who had never made it into exile and had known unremitting and horrendous suffering for almost forty years by then. When they heard me speaking Tibetan, people would rush toward me to tell me their stories. Their parents, brothers, sisters, aunts, uncles, nephews, children had been arrested, tortured, imprisoned, beaten, maimed, and killed. Their temples had been dismantled, their family rosaries destroyed, their lamas clubbed to death in front of their eyes. They would urge me, "Tell the world what you have seen here! Give this letter of mine to His Holiness, to

President Reagan, to the U.N." The emotions were so deep, it was impossible for me not to weep while they told me their troubles.

In 1989, Nena became dangerously ill and our whole family went into crisis mode. A few days after visiting what some thought might have been her deathbed, His Holiness was awarded the Nobel Peace Prize. It was an amazing year: Czechoslovakia, East Germany, and Poland were liberated; the Soviet Union began to dissolve. There was an apocalypse in our family and in the world. Fortunately, Nena soon made a miraculous recovery.

Thinking more than ever about the persisting agony of Tibet, I was at the same time tremendously buoyed up by the positive changes in the world, as well as by the West's growing awareness of Buddhism. The strange thing about the messianic ideal of liberating yourself so that you can free all others is that just trying to adopt it makes you feel happier. Even though you know on some level that there is only so much you can get done in any given period of time, the fact that you do not let go of the determination to do everything gives you immense good cheer. This, I found, was the source of Geshe Wangyal's peace, the bottomless kindness of my teachers in India, and probably the cause of the smile on the Vietnamese monk's face as he was consumed by the flames.

Our lives remain a bundle of contradictions. We have a hard time living up to our own ideals, but in 1990, with Nena recovering and His Holiness wielding the Nobel Peace

Prize, it seemed as if anything were possible, now that the senseless destructiveness of the Cold War was coming to an end, against all bets.

The tradition of nonviolence, optimism, concern for the individual, and unconditional compassion that developed in Tibet is the culmination of a slow inner revolution, a cool one, hard to see, that began 2,500 years ago with the Buddha's insight about the end of suffering. What I have learned from these people has forever changed my life, and I believe their culture contains an inner science particularly relevant to the difficult time in which we live. My desire is to share some of the profound hope for our future that they have shared with me.

INTRODUCTION

*T*here is a story that 2,500 years ago, while he was giving a teaching, the Buddha placed his big toe pointedly
on the earth and with that dramatic gesture revealed to an
audience that the universe we live in is pure paradise. Not
that what we see normally is the best of all possible worlds,
as Voltaire's Candide tried to convince himself, but that if we
understood the true nature of reality, we would see the
planet we live on as the perfect theater for positive evolution
that it truly is.

A pure land is the environment created by a fully enlightened being so that as many others as possible have the
potential also for developing into fully enlightened beings.
This enlightened individual is called a buddha. Shakyamuni
Buddha was not simply an historical figure who lived and
taught 2,500 years ago—he is an example of the full flowering of human potential, reached by undergoing inner rev-

olutions, coups of the spirit in which the power of negative impulses and emotions is toppled and we are freed to be as happy, good, and compassionate as we can evolve to be. The Buddha developed an inner science for achieving this revolution, one that was preserved in Tibet after invaders nearly wiped it out of India 1,000 years ago. Since Tibet was built on the foundation that a society's top priority is to provide all the means for each individual to achieve this inner revolution, Tibet is our toehold for seeing where inner revolution might lead, giving us a glimpse of the architectural plans for building that pure land revealed by the Buddha's toe pointing.

Internationally renowned biologist Rupert Sheldrake has a theory he calls "morphic resonance." Sheldrake hypothesizes that an individual's or group's actions, beliefs, and insights create resonances that make it more likely that other people, otherwise unconnected and unaware of the thoughts or occurrences, will experience the same events or insights as if spontaneously on their own. If I have an insight, the theory goes, people around me are more likely to experience something similar, even if I do not tell them about it. Sheldrake's views are controversial, but they make intuitive sense, and experimental data is beginning to prove him right.

Our empirical bent leaves us incredulous in the face of this sort of possibility. Consider, however, the phenomena of radio, television, and microwave transmissions. Their signals are generated as patterns in subtle energy fields that move out in broadcast patterns which hang in the air, so to speak. None of us can see, hear, or feel them, but if a receiver with the proper components is constructed, the raw pattern can be translated back into sounds and images, a radio voice, a television image. We take this for granted, clicking on and tuning in with no sense of mystery or wonder.

The human brain is an amazingly complex transmission and receiving device. Its hundred billion neurons must be sensitive to many things our outer bodily senses cannot discern. Sensory stimuli are translated for us through complex software programming, which enables us to recognize the percepts—the images we perceive as familiar objects—and to have ideas, to see internal images, hear internal voices, have profound feelings, and so forth. Once certain programs have become routine in our brains, we can articulate those programs to other people through language, image, song, rhythm, or a multitude of other means. Why might we not also radiate the patterns of those programs so that they can "hang in the air" and be directly received by other brains? How many times, for example, have we found ourselves commenting on a friend's statement, "I was just about to say the same thing"?

Our involvement with others does not begin with just our speech and physical movements. Each of us individually has an effect on the lives of beings around us through the quiet processes going on in our minds. If we are full of good feelings, they radiate around us and people want to be near. If we are full of bad feelings, others tend to stay away. So if we would be activists for good, for the positive, we must assume responsibility for our minds as well as our speech and our physical activities, otherwise our negative mental habits will drag down the entire community of beings. On the other hand, when we break through into the liberty of heart, mind, and spirit in the process of enlightenment, we free others at the same time.

We can envision the planet as the residence of billions of human beings each living around a bubble of inner awareness, each having an inner theater of sounds and lights and impulses that is interconnected with everyone else's through broadcast vibrations and patterns. When one of those bubbles explodes in a burst of insight or joy—when it releases a knot in its interior energy circulation—it influences ever so slightly all the other bubbles. When an educational, cultural, or civilizational movement influences a large number of those bubbles in certain ways, an even more powerful resonance which affects all the other bubbles is created. If we see morphic resonance as a principle operating in history, we can conceive of the possibility that when a whole country or a group of countries adopts a new pattern of perception or behavior, surrounding countries can be profoundly influenced as well.

The enlightenment movement's inner revolution has, for

the 2,500 years since the Buddha's emergence, acted as a subtle wave rippling through the ocean of bubbles that is the world of beings. During the enlightenment process, each individual bubble becomes aware of the totality of its own potential and of its resonance with and support of all other bubbles. When a bubble goes through the enlightening unfoldment, it stimulates a parallel experience in so many bubbles that it brings an era of spiritual growth to the planet. Think about the world during the sixth century B.C.E., when the Buddha's bubble burst into enlightenment. Zoroaster had revolutionized Iranian religion; Deutero-Isaiah and his colleagues were beginning to codify five books of Moses; Socrates was soon to educate the youth of Athens; Confucius was setting down the code for Chinese civilization, and Lao Tzu was providing spiritual relief from it; and Buddha's India was seething with creativity. Historian Arnold Toynbee has called this period the Axial Age—it was pivotal for all Eurasian civilizations. Such waves have occurred since, driving parallel spurts of spiritual growth in India and Tibet and worldwide. In our time of nearly limitless communication and freedom of choice in so many countries, our civilization is ripe for another step in what the Buddha saw as our inevitable evolution toward happiness.

The Buddha's enlightenment movement sought from the beginning to take power from the ruling bodies and return it to the individual. The Buddha found that inner freedom—freedom from our negative emotions and obsessive self-concern—is the essential precondition for goodness and social liberty. As a result, the enlightenment movement often takes a countercultural stance. Think of the Buddhist monks and nuns tortured by the communist Chinese government, or the Vietnamese Buddhist monk who immolated himself to get the attention of governments gone mad with killing. Enlightenment education provides a critique of authoritarian ideas that frees the individual from unquestioning obedience. Such inner freedom tends to be feared by centralized governments. Even in our time, the early proponents of Buddhism and the freedom of mind it encourages were nonconformists: Henry David Thoreau, and beat writers such as Allen Ginsberg and Jack Kerouac.

At times the enlightenment movement was integrated into an existing culture. Many kings of India and other prosperous regions of Asia welcomed it with open arms. They turned to it to help them in developing their own peace of mind, to help keep harmony, to serve as an ethical and educational foundation for national prosperity and positive development. Often, enlightenment principles became central in a polity, producing numerous enlightened citizens, beautiful works of art, wonderful festivals and events.

Usually this process would be arrested by the intrusion of some outside force, since enlightenment movements inevitably lead to gentleness and relative disarmament.

The peaceful influence of meditative realization on a civilization has the two-sided effect of making that society happier, wealthier, gentler, but also militarily weaker—an attractive target for aggressive outsiders. In most longer-lived enlightenment-oriented societies, the ruler preserved an army to defend the country while supporting a second society within the nation built around a monastic university, where individuals could safely disarm and pursue enlightenment. These two societies would then coexist in tension, maintaining an uneasy balance.

Tibet represents the sole exception to this pattern. Just as the Indian tectonic plate is still rolling under the Asian plate and pushing the Himalayas and the Tibetan plateau higher every year, so the enlightenment tradition of India turned away from the devastation wrought by the series of conquests India suffered at the end of the first millennium c.e. and climbed over the Himalayan wall into Tibet, where its energy found sanctuary and a fertile environment to thrive so that we could meet this living tradition a thousand years later. When the enlightenment movement hit Tibet, the process of disarmament proceeded rapidly. Tibet's militaristic dynasty, which originally had imported Buddhism in the eighth century, foundered after a few hundred years, never again revived, and the country was more or less vulnerable to outsiders from then on. Without an army to oppose them, it might have been expected that Chinese, Indic, Iranian, or Central Asian peoples previously raided and oppressed by Tibetan armies would seek revenge. But for the special geography of Tibet, this certainly would have happened. It was the least accessible place, protected by the Himalayas, and once there, an army would be hard put to survive in the harsh climate of the highest plateau in the world.

There was, at the turn of the first millennium, very little wealth to be taken from Tibet: Agricultural production, while sufficient for a small, balanced population, could never compete with rich alluvial growing seasons elsewhere; the considerable mineral wealth was too difficult to extract in quantity; and wool, meat, rare herbs, milk products, and salt were brought down from the plateau by Tibetan traders, who were much better equipped to collect and transport such products across the treacherous mountains than any invading armies. No one, until modern times, wanted to conquer, colonize, or incorporate Tibet.

Tibet's material scarcity contributed to its spiritual evolution. Physical hardships, if not too severe, can intensify people's development of compassion as well as their drive to see beyond the material world. Thus Tibet became a laboratory for the enlightenment movement to create its model society, to evolve into an actual manifestation of a buddha's pure universe, a "buddhaverse." A social buddhaverse is a place where everything is geared toward enlightenment, where every lifetime is made meaningful by dedication to optimal evolutionary development.

Because that nation embraced the enlightenment movement for more than a millennium, Tibet is the prime example of a sustained attempt by an entire people to create a
society, culture, and civilization that cherish the individual's
pursuit of enlightenment over the needs of society. Instead
of believing that a strong central government can force a
group of people into making a better place to live, the Tibetans, influenced by ancient India, saw that helping the individual is what transforms society. Imagine a culture in
which everything is geared toward helping all individuals
become the best human beings they can be; in which individuals are driven to devoting their lives to becoming enlightened by the natural flood of compassion for others that
arises from their wisdom. Once an individual attains enlightenment, society at large automatically becomes enriched. This principle was the heart of the Buddha's social
revolution. This does not mean that Tibet is or ever was perfect, or that the whole world should become like Tibet. But
Tibet is unique, and we can learn from its example.

Like India before it, Tibet influenced the rest of the world
in ways that may seem obscure or unlikely to us, weaned as
we have been on history as a chain of material events. But
again, if you examine global civilization as Tibet began to
manifest as an "enlightenment factory" in the fourteenth century, you will see a similar worldwide pattern. With this
powerful release of a people's energy, a great renaissance
began, a flowering of human achievement that may well have

transmitted a subtle inspiration for people all around the world. At the same time Tibet opened its heart fully to pacifist monks and nuns spending their days in learning, meditation, and creativity, there was a major shift in the West that led to the Renaissance. During that time, power was taken from the Church and given back to the individual—a new confidence in human reason and human enterprise was born.

Unlike in the modern West, where efforts are directed outwardly, toward material progress, in Tibet, energies were directed inwardly, toward progress in the development of an inner universe, toward spiritual progress. The soul was thought of as a subtle, relative, totally and inextricably interconnected process, powerfully influencing and influenced by its environment. So it was the soul that mattered, the soul that was to be developed. It was the soul that needed industry, investment, cultivation.

At the same time, the Western Renaissance began to restore man to the center of things, spreading from Italy the confidence in reason that was to bring forth the Western Enlightenment. This Enlightenment was characterized by a new perception of enlightened human genius as being in line with the natural strong force of the universe, stimulated by the rediscovery of the ancients' faith in the powers of the human being. As in Tibet, this kind of self-confidence liberated energy for personal evolution and made possible the progressive development of science, great achievements in the arts, and a higher level of personal energy for the individual in daily life.

Our historical habit is to think of this period as the rise of the West, the time when the turn to reason and science linked itself with European aggressiveness and adventurousness to produce world empires and the industrial revolution. We tend to think that this drive toward what I call outer modernity was produced by basic values unique to European civilization. European Christendom, in arising as conqueror of the entire planet, thus showed what it assumed to be its innate superiority over other cultures around the world. But from another perspective, the relative self-restraint of Asian civilizations that were influenced by the enlightenment movement—as in China's decision not to use its newly invented gunpowder for conquest—looks far wiser that the modern West's course, which has led to the proliferation of weapons capable of destroying the world.

By the seventeenth century, Tibet had achieved the modern form of its society by means of its unique social and psychological creation, which I call inner, or spiritual, modernity, an exact mirror image of the outer, or secular, modernity just taking off in the Western Enlightenment. The key attribute of both modernities is the unification of psyche and society by overcoming the sacred/secular duality. The West collapsed the sacred into the secular, disenchanting everything through materialism, while Tibet transformed the secular into the sacred, seeing through matter and discovering the nuclear energy of the mind. Whichever the direction, the unification itself released an enormous energy for change. The West spread its outer industrial revolution worldwide, physically conquering and transforming the planet. Tibet intensified its inner industrial revolution, developing industrial-strength mass monasteries in which individuals conquered their innermost energies and transformed their world into a buddhaverse.

Though spiritually highly developed, the people of Tibet knew they were not in Shangrila, not in a final utopia or a heavenly buddhaverse. They knew there were many violent and ignorant potentials within their own psyches; they knew they were not free from their own egocentric lust and hate. They saw great pockets of problems in their own culture and society, and were aware of the threats still present from the ancient primitive structures of the violent Tibet of their past. But the main direction of the society was ecstatic and positive; intrigues, violence, and persecution were rarer there than in any other civilization.

The inner modernity of Tibet's enlightenment-dedicated civilization flourished for more than three hundred years. While Tibet turned inward politically, the great empires of the West and East conquered the rest of the world, and unified most of it culturally as well, using the engine of industrial production and the tools of modern warfare, transport, and communication.

But the technologies and institutions of conquest and unification prove extremely ill-suited to the maintenance of harmony and creativity within one global society. Outer modernity by itself seems to require a continuously expanding frontier, an area for the safe ventilating of the un-

tamed wildness of the involuntary emotions of an uninte-
grated subconscious. Inner modernity by itself seems to require socially isolated laboratory conditions to keep it from
being smothered by the outer modern conquest. What may
look on the surface like steady, stable progress toward a
global modernism modeled on the United States is really a
deeply unstable world with widespread suffering. Our twentieth century has been almost one long holocaust of world
wars and local genocidal conflicts, with the largest losses of
life being caused by huge bureaucratic governments systematically exterminating their own subjects.

To understand the world wars of this century—not just
the two known with the capital letters but the whole violent
holocaust of the fall of the empires, the wars of liberation,
the clash of ideologies, and the Cold War, with its numerous
hot proxy wars—we must look at the entire phenomenon of
the conquest of the planet and the industrial subjugation of
its peoples. If we look at the rise of outer modernity through
the eyes of a nonparticipant—whether a member of the enlightenment movement or a tribesman, a Lakota warrior, a
Mongolian herdsman—it does not seem at all to be a triumph of human ingenuity or a wonderful culmination of
human progress. Rather, it appears as a demonic invasion, an
irascible fate allowing certain tribes, or nations, access to a
level of destructive magic that threatens to push the tribe/
tribe balance and the human/nature balance into terminal
disequilibrium.

———

Society is made up of individuals whose collective interest is no more than the sum of their individual interests, one by one. No matter how much territory the society acquires, how much glory, how much wealth, how much productivity and prosperity, each individual within it still will sicken, age, and die. The collective cannot help that individual beyond death. Only individuals' enlightenment—their clear knowledge of their own minds, conscious, instinctual, and subtle—and their confident mastery of their deepest reactions can assist them in their onward journey. As the enlightenment of each one individually is the most important thing for each one, so the enlightenment of any one individual is of supreme importance at any one time.

Buddhist writings describe celestial realms of pure light, pure bliss. Beings there can contemplate at leisure and attain deep states of concentration and wisdom. But they lack the spur that one's own suffering and the suffering of others gives to developing compassion. Without the dynamic of compassion, they lack the impetus to evolve to the perfection of buddhahood, to the summit of evolution, the state of total freedom. We need challenges to keep us vital. Unless we are already enlightened, sitting around being blissful leads to stagnation and decadence. And this is why it is better to be born in our world of ordinary suffering than in a lotus land.

This is not an argument against creating a buddhaversal human society. Anywhere in the human realm, suffering, ignorance, and death will never be far away, no matter how pleasant the conditions of a particular society. Even if we make a local society relatively happy and peaceful, there is a planet full of miserable others we will have to reach out to and assist. Even if we were to develop cosmic abilities and make the entire planet into a place where the greatest number could evolve with the greatest efficiency toward evolutionary fulfillment and happiness, we then would be faced with sustaining that process as well as liberating all the other species of animals from their suffering.

Tibet may seem a small and insignificant country in the larger scheme of things, but Tibetan civilization at the time of the Chinese invasion in 1950 was the result of 2,500 years of the revolutionary development of enlightenment culture. This revolution produced a population of people who were broadly determined to live for positive evolutionary transformation. Tibet is an important example for the world, and its restoration as a region of peace and spirituality is a matter of global significance. Tibet's unique focus on enlightenment civilization makes that nation crucial to the world's development of spiritual and social balance.

For nearly forty years now, the Fourteenth Dalai Lama has led the preservation of the inner modernity of Tibet within the refugee enclaves of India while simultaneously guiding the Tibetans in a quick and successful adaptation to outer modernity. He has gone back to the root of the enlightenment tradition and elaborated a viable path of nonviolent activism, building a community that represents inner modernity confronting outer modernity. Almost alone among the leaders of peoples under genocidal attack, he has consistently refused to turn to violence to solve his problems.

We are aware of the power of brainwashing to develop fanaticism and hatred, but we fail to respect the power of positive conditioning to systematically develop openness of mind, altruistic compassion, and joyous love. We are happy when people are generous, peaceful, and loving, but we think it a surprise, an aberration from the norm of self-concern. We know that the many problems of the environment, human societies, and the international community can never be solved unless individuals and groups come to a better understanding of their situations, voluntarily change their ways, and do the right things without being forced into it. When we see positive behavior as abnormal, we lose hope, unable to comprehend why people would get a kick out of benevolence or why they would find satisfaction in giving up something to which they might have clung.

The Dalai Lama argues that human determination is more powerful than bullets. He leads his nation in a movement for liberation through nonviolence despite the special burdens of an international liberation movement led from exile rather than a revolution within a nation. His people are a minority now in their own country, and the oppressor a vast majority.

The Chinese have the ability to exclude all international media from Tibet whenever they wish, making a campaign of liberation through information and consciousness-raising especially difficult.

Our whole secularized world is built on apocalyptic consciousness: The end of history is constantly being announced, caused by this or that relatively short-term trend. We want to live for the now, we want total personal power and energy, we want immediate fruition. But is our millennium complete? Did we realize the kingdom of God on earth, or did we just settle for a kingdom of earth by giving up the very idea of a kingdom of God? How do we discover a higher unity by reconciling the heaven/earth duality instead of trying to choose one and deny the other? The Buddha's inner revolution gives us some long-overlooked insights into this most central question.

Chapter 1

AWAKENING

*H*istorians see the mid–first millennium B.C.E. as a time of massive militarism, the time of the Trojan wars in the Mediterranean, the Mahabharata wars in India, the disintegration of the Chou dynasty in China. Societies all over Eurasia and North Africa had reached the stage of city-state militaristic rivalry, midway on the long journey from local tribalisms toward regional imperialisms. New breakthroughs in iron technology had allowed agriculture to flourish and create surpluses to sustain large cities with full-time professional armies, which enabled the warrior clans that occupied the thrones to wage long, bloody, genocidal, year-round wars instead of the occasional tribal clashes their ethic was developed for. The new cities developed stratified societies, with oppressive elites controlling large, alienated masses. Priestly orders legitimated the warrior dynasties, using private rituals that excluded the majority from a sense of religious participation.

On the other hand, the mercantile and artisan classes were gaining in wealth and power. They were looking for new ideas, were supporting new teachers, and were open to new religious and philosophical wisdom. Wandering ascetics, holy men, and philosophers traveled from town to town, questioning the old myths and traditions. They championed the power of reason and the importance of the individual quest. They challenged the violent honor codes of the kings, the elitism of religious ideas and practices, and the validity of the social hierarchy. The world was ripe for a new, critically deepened understanding of causation, of evolution, of the purpose of life. It was time for a new possibility for human happiness and evolutionary fulfillment, and many people hoped for the appearance of a fully awakened being, a buddha, to lead them.

The traditional mythic accounts of the Buddha's life begin with his descent from one heaven to another. He arose from his state of ecstatic rest on the boundary between infinity and form to take reincarnation through magical apparition as a prince of gods in the brilliant Tushita heaven. While living there, he spent most of his time teaching the liberating truth to the vast host abiding there. He also observed the creatures of earth, trying to see if he could help. He conversed with learned sages about the best circumstances in which to reincarnate to fulfill his mission of liberating all beings from the sufferings of unawakened living. A moment of time in the Tushita heaven corresponds to years on earth, so he remained alert to pick his era, nation, continent, social class, family, sex, and so on for optimal impact. He eventually picked the male form in the royal family of the Indian Shakya nation, around what we would call 563 B.C.E.

The Buddha decided that the most effective social class for him would be the royal or warrior class. His earthshaking demonstration of the vanity of mundane ways thus would have the greatest impact—from this topmost class, he would have access to all the power of his society and then abandon it as worthless with respect to the ultimate purpose of human life. The Buddha's actions marked the beginning of a special kind of revolution—a cool revolution, not a hot, violent one—that continues as a gradual process of civilization that for all its slowness is steady in its progress and sure in its ultimate success.

All the images of the Buddha's birth and youth symbolically announce a major shift in civilization. He is described as having been conceived while his mother, Mayadevi, was on retreat, away from his father or any male, and then born in a blooming, springtime garden while Mayadevi was away from her husband's palace. When the infant Buddha was presented in an ancestral temple, the god-images came to life, stepped down from their pedestals, and bowed in obeisance to him. He was named Siddhartha, "He who accomplishes his goal," and the sages predicted that he would be either an all-powerful world emperor or a perfectly enlightened world teacher. Naturally he was brought up to become a world-conquering emperor. His royal father, Shuddhodana, had a solid ambition that his son should rule the world, so he could not imagine any use for a perfectly enlightened being.

Siddhartha became a top student, a powerful athlete, and an accomplished prince, yet he showed a special gentleness and nobility that worried his father. He was wed to a beautiful and noble girl, Yashodhara, the daughter of a warrior, and the young couple lived blissfully for ten years in a continuous round of pleasure. In one story they make love so enthusiastically that in their absorption they fall off a pavilion roof and land softly in a flower bed without taking notice. Eventually, Yashodhara gave birth to a beautiful boy. In the social custom of the time, the birth of a grandson signaled a king's retirement in favor of his son, who then would serve the kingdom until his son had a son. Siddhartha was proclaimed crown prince, and the date of his coronation was set.

But Prince Siddhartha had become radically discontent, ready to revolt against being bound by social duty. While out driving in the city, he saw four disturbing sights from which he previously had been sheltered: an old person, a sick person, a dead body, and the inspiring countenance of an ascetic sage. He returned home to his father and asked him for the secret of protecting their people from old age, sickness, death, and suffering. Shuddhodana responded that it was not the business of kings; that rulers dealt with economy, law, foreign policy, defense, and so forth; that no one could solve those other problems; and that they simply went to the priests for help in dealing with such matters. Siddhartha announced that he would not be content to rule until he found the way to eliminate this suffering. He asked his father's permission to retire from the world to seek enlightenment in a forest retreat. The king denied his request, posted guards around the prince's palaces, and advanced the day of the coronation.

Then came the great renunciation, Siddhartha's resolution to abandon wife and child, father and kingdom, his own duty, identity, and property in order to pursue the meaning of living. He was willing to rupture the traditional social fabric to set off on what seemed a lost cause. Siddhartha looked upon his infant son, sleeping with his beloved wife, and silently said good-bye. He had to escape from the city by stealth, for his father had a triple guard on all gates.

The following day, having discovered Siddhartha's flight, Yashodhara held up their infant son and cried out how hardhearted Siddhartha was to have abandoned them like that. Shuddhodana was crushed. He sent out ministers and high priests to track down Siddhartha in the jungle and talk him into coming back. The king had reason, duty, and custom on his side. Siddhartha had nothing but vague ancient precedents and a grim determination to do the impossible—to understand the entire nature of life and death and to find a way out of suffering so he could teach it to others.

Siddhartha crossed the river and entered the jungle, cut off his long princely hair with a stroke of his sword, and gave his jewels to his groom. He traded his royal robes for an ascetic's garment of cremation shrouds. After rejecting the teachings he discovered at various ashrams, he set out with five companions and lived for six years in the jungle doing extreme ascetic practices, sometimes eating no more than a grain of rice a day. He became totally emaciated and fanatically taut with determination, yet still he did not reach his goal of freedom from suffering.

Siddhartha eventually came to the insight that too much self-torture was just as counterproductive as too much self-indulgence. Either way led to obsession with the body and its states of being. He saw that if he was to come to a precise understanding of the reality of the deepest self, he would need to confront it clearly. In order for him to be able to do so, his body would need to be relatively comfortable. He gave up asceticism, bathed, ate, and went to sit under a giant fig tree near the town of Bodhgaya. He sat down in the late afternoon, saying, "Here I will sit and will not move from this spot until my work is done; until I have awakened to the perfect enlightenment; until all is clear and calm and the way is certain." According to the story, the earth quaked gently, the wind sighed. All beings throughout the planet felt a stirring of anticipation, a shiver of joy.

Night fell; Siddhartha still sat and in a lucid state reviewed millions of former lives, the infinite struggles of all the beings he'd ever encountered, endless possible future scenarios, and the myriad arts needed to actualize the best scenarios. Just before Siddhartha achieved buddhahood, Mara, the devil himself, appeared and debated with him: "How can you claim to be a perfect buddha? By what right? Are you overly proud?" Siddhartha responded by telling the evil one of the numberless acts of enormous self-sacrifice, of outstanding creativity and transcendent wisdom that he remembered performing in his former lives, which now made possible his becoming a buddha. Mara retorted, "That's all very well, but who is your witness? No one but you remembers this, so who will believe you?" The Buddha made his famous gesture of reaching down with his right hand to touch mother earth, and said, "I call the earth herself to witness. She has borne me in all those billions of lives. She has seen it all. She will testify for me." The earth manifested sixteen forest goddesses, who stood in a circle and recited the tales of the Buddha's former lives—his great heroism, his great accomplishments, his great gifts, his great ordeals. The scenes themselves unfolded before Mara's eyes as the stories were told. Mara was deeply moved aesthetically, connoisseur of literature and drama that he is, and then, remembering his purpose, petulantly vanished from the scene, teleporting back to his own realm to think of some revenge.

Siddhartha continued to sit, persevering in his quest, and by the next morning attained the perfect understanding that freed him from suffering. He was renamed Shakyamuni, "Sage of the Shakyas." He saw the path his work would take and felt the art for liberating beings surge forth. He stayed put for a while, enjoying his new blissful wisdom, then arose to spend the next forty-five years teaching people in all levels of society in all lands accessible to him.

He founded a revolution, not a violent one that makes things worse for everyone, but a cool, slow, effective revolution that can make people's full liberation a reality. In his teaching he confronted the forces of negativity directly and precisely. He showed power to the powerful, gentleness to the meek, wisdom to the intelligent, passion and heart to the simple and good-hearted. He established a large and expanding community of enlightenment seekers. Then, when he was older than eighty, he withdrew his adherence to his bodily form. He did this because the community was on its way to becoming securely established and even powerful, and it was more healthy for it that he remove his personal authority. He wanted to make it clear that he intended people to be free.

When he attained the buddha state, Shakyamuni is reported to have said: "Profound, peaceful, uncomplicated, transparent, and uncreated—I have found a truthlike elixir of immortality!"

What did he mean by this? Profound is the truth discovered at the absolute depth of things; it is reached by the ultimate penetration of all superficial realities, the result of a quest that goes beyond death and life, beyond pain and pleasure. Peaceful is the truth that stands alone; it is a final reality that cannot be changed, since it incorporates all changes. Uncomplicated is the truth that one encompasses without agitation. Transparent is the truth where knower and known are one, where light and beauty are everywhere, even in apparent darkness and horror. Uncreated is the truth that is not made, that has always been, and will always be. It is the safe refuge, the true home, the long-sought goal, the supreme bliss. To discover it is to drink an elixir of immortality. It fills up every atom of one's being with happiness, ecstasy, relief, and security. This truth transforms death into bliss, and life into fearless freedom. It is what lies behind the Buddha's smile.

What was it that Buddha discovered? What did he start? What can be said with some certainty is that it was not a religion. A young seeker who would later become one of the Buddha's most famous disciples met an old monk on the streets of the Indian city of Varanasi whose composure and contented glow were notable. The youth asked the old mendicant about his teacher and the teaching he followed. The monk avowed inability to explain and invited the seeker to visit his teacher, the Buddha. The seeker insisted on some explanation, and the monk said, "OM! The Transcendent Lord said that all things arise from causes, what are their causes, and what their cessation. Such being his philosophy, hail the Great Wanderer!" This mantralike statement contains the core insight of Buddhism. It is essentially a scientific proclamation of observable cause, effect, and the cessation of negative causality. Who ever became pious about causes and cessations?

The Buddha's era has been called the Axial Age, since at that time there was a shift in thinking that occurred in variant forms in widely divergent cultures. The great innovation was the attention paid to causation: It is found in the writings of Hippocrates the doctor, Plato the philosopher, Confucius the ethical philosopher, and in many Indian works. The older, mythic, prerational cosmos explained events in terms of the will of the gods. When afflicted with sickness, troubled by events, hemmed in by enemies, one consulted ritual specialists to discover how one had offended the gods. The rational approach just coming into vogue insisted that the gods did not control life; that everything was subject to discernible causes; and that once these causes were clearly understood, the situation could be changed by intervening in the processes of causation.

The Buddha's elucidation of causation—how myriad causes and conditions underlie everything—applies throughout all realms of experience, natural, physical, moral, emotional, spiritual. This theory of evolution, called karma, is based on the idea that one's good fortune arises as the direct result of one's good actions in the past, and one's misfortunes from one's bad actions. It is often understood simplistically as the notion that one good or bad turn elicits another, like an echo. It is actually far more subtle, describing neither a random, meaningless universe nor a deterministic universe where one is at the mercy of malevolent gods. It is analogous to the Darwinian theory of natural selection, with one key difference: Darwin's concept focuses on the physical evolution of species; karma focuses on both the physical and the spiritual progress of individual beings, who evolve throughout an infinite but continuous process of physical lifetimes. In the Darwinian context, we see our physical evolution, our survival of the fittest, as tantamount to survival of the meanest. If that were so, why have we developed such delicate, soft hands instead of giant claws? In the karmic system, one kind of action is systematically more successful than another in enhancing a being's existence. That action is compassion, and one look at our hands—which seem more suited to gentleness than to violence—tells the whole story. A being develops a propensity for this constructive action over many lifetimes, and the pursuit of that course leads to changes in the being's actual form of embodiment.

In Darwinian natural selection, biological evolutionary development happens over many generations of species and is spread among the members of each species, the successful results of the action being carried from individual to individual by genetic encoding. In karmic evolution, development happens over many generations of an individual continuum embodied as a member of different species in life-form after life-form. The successful results of the action are carried from individual life to individual life by encoding in a "spiritual gene." This is the subtle, instinctual soul-pattern that bears the vague traces of previous experiences through the death-rebirth transition, leaving the gross body and brain at death, going through a dreamlike transitional period, and gravitating through habitual propensity toward a new embodiment in a womb.

In karmic evolution, the successful actions that lead to positive evolutionary mutations such as a human life are those of generosity, morality, tolerance, enterprise, concentration, and intelligence. Their opposites—stinginess, injustice, anger, laziness, distraction, and ignorance—are unsuccessful actions, which lead to negative evolutionary mutations that take you down the chain through animal incarnations. Saving others' lives broadens one's scope of relationships, strengthens one by connecting with the reciprocal goodwill of others, and enhances one's awareness of life's potential. Killing others, though it might achieve a short-term goal of providing safety, food, or property, narrows one's scope of relationships, weakens one by cutting off others' goodwill, and cuts down one's awareness of life, increasing paranoia. Over many lives, killing turns one into a Tyrannosaurus-type being, while saving lives turns one into a human, the form that has the greatest potential for buddhahood. This emphasis on understanding causation so that bad situations can be remedied is the hallmark of the Buddha's teaching.

His cardinal teaching of the Four Noble Truths—that there is suffering, a cause of suffering, a cessation to suffering, and a path to that cessation—is basically a causal diagnosis and prescription. Our pains are sufferings, obviously. Our ordinary pleasures seem the opposite, but the seeker of enlightenment knows that they bring suffering by being fleeting and addictive, leaving us more discontent when we lose them than if we never had them. Our very existence is suffering in that it inevitably awaits destruction. Our birth is a suffering, as we are crushed in the birth canal and hurled helpless into the world. Babies emerge crying, after all, not laughing. Our sicknesses are sufferings. Our decay is always suffering. Our deaths are sufferings. Meeting with the unloved is suffering, and parting with the beloved is suffering.

We may have a hard time believing that our lives bring nothing but suffering, but we might be stirred to look more closely. It is not that we are meant to resign ourselves to a suffering that we cannot escape. On the contrary, we are instructed that the misery of life, when faced, inspires us to make the effort to escape its suffering.

The second truth, following closely on the first, is that our suffering has an origin. This origin lies in our misunderstanding of reality. This idea is simple: Each of us thinks that he or she is the center of the universe, essentially an independent, separate awareness, apart from all other persons and things. Feeling small and alienated is what drives us to acquire friends, lovers, and possessions—they provide buffers against what we think of as the vast "other." As long as we remain convinced that we are separate from a world we conceive as set against us, we are bound to be frustrated in our desires, bound to lose our battle against such overwhelming odds. Vulnerable to injury, we are quick to fear and anger, wanting to destroy things before they destroy us. Our actions cause harm to others and to ourselves through their negative evolutionary effects upon our lives. Thus we can come to the realization that our mistaken understanding of being terminally isolated is inherently ineffective.

The third noble fact is the truth of cessation, or freedom. Often people have thought that Buddha was a pessimist because of his harping on suffering. But suffering is only one of four facts. It is merely the confrontation with the symptom. The reason the Buddha smiled is that he found the third noble fact, freedom from suffering. This freedom is attained by facing the suffering first, and then by understanding and abandoning its origin.

The fourth noble fact is that there is an eightfold path to freedom from suffering. Freedom cannot be realized instantaneously. We can't change our habits of mind in the blink of an eye because our instinctual propensity for delusion, hatred, and desire is powerful and long-standing. The cultivation of ethics and meditative awareness reconditions our delusory ideas and addictive drives. Developing the wisdom penetrating the nature of reality and implementing the eight branches completes the process: authentic view, right motivation, mindfulness, right speech, right industry, right ac-

tion, right livelihood, and meditation. Besides needing teachers and friends to help travel this path, one needs social permission through the establishment of institutions that foster
the development of the eight branches. In this simple structure of Buddha's basic prescription for his contemporaries,
we can see the foundation of the cultural and social revolution he engineered.

Thus, the enlightenment movement does not fit the normal definition of a religion. A religion is based on a belief system that mandates a certain pattern of ritual actions, social
structures, and ethical norms. Buddha taught the need for
freedom from belief systems in order to develop the power
of critical wisdom. He taught the relativity of social structures and the supremacy of the individual's right to freedom. And he taught that the scientific understanding of
reality naturally leads to effective ethical behavior. His was an
educational movement affecting not only individuals but
whole cultures, entire systems of thinking and living.

Once you come to the perspective of life as beginningless
and endless, then taking your instincts and habits in hand
and cultivating generosity, justice, patience, discipline, concentration, and critical wisdom to a degree sufficient for the
radical evolutionary transformation called enlightenment no
longer seems remote. The project is simply a systematic attempt to discover the true nature of reality, clear that the full

knowledge of reality will be radically transforming. We spend years being educated about reality as it is taught in our schools. In the quest for enlightenment, we simply extend that education by dislodging all preconceived limitations on our ability to know.

We tend to think of enlightenment as a distant cognitive state, either an intensely stressful intellectual comprehension of a huge number of physical facts that a computer could handle just as well, or a semiobliterated state of mystical transcendence better left to denizens of the margins of society. We think selflessness is a state of martyrdom, a religious frenzy of self-destruction, unhealthy physically as well as psychologically. Our operative psychologies teach that the habitual ego-centered self is the only one there is, so they reinforce our enslavement to its demands for comfort, stability, and consumption.

We become enlightened when we see through our blinding misperception. Through examination we see the once-rigid ego dissolve into fiction, and the solidity of our world turns fluid. In that lightness of the transparent self, we feel a new connectedness with the world. Freedom from enslavement to the ego as center of the universe becomes the bliss of union with the free-flowing energy of the world. Beyond the tense pacts, conflicts, or standoffs between "I" and "you," "they," or "it," there is a liberated "we" flexibly interacting on the field of total freedom.

The word "enlightenment" is a good equivalent for "buddhahood" because it is both the intellectual accomplishment and the spiritual experience of complete awakening. Enlightenment is more than cognitive; it is emotional and moral, since the openness of wisdom brings happiness, which automatically releases the most positive emotions and generates benevolent actions.

Enlightenment is attained by the body as well as the mind. The mind may gain enlightenment even in an instant of transcendent experience, but the body's enlightenment, which concerns the fulfillment of one's altruistic interests as well as one's self-interest, is a gradual and evolutionary process. Enlightenment is the product of a long cultivation of a body perfectly fitted to the communication of enlightenment to all other beings. Through a process of evolution over many lives, a person's mind, speech, and even physical body become perfect instruments for helping others. Enlightenment is the summit of human evolution.

Although enlightenment includes transcendent states, those states are nothing in themselves if not simultaneously the fountainhead of energetic compassion directed at all beings. Intellectually conceived compassion always fails to complete its purpose, since its sensitivity is always constrained by less than total openness to the raw nature of reality. Unconditional compassion, on the other hand, accomplishes whatever is needed to make beings happy.

We have trouble conceiving ourselves as buddhas because we are used to thinking that the way we are is the only way we can be. To open our minds at least to the possibility of enlightenment, we must dig out the presuppositions that make it hard for us to imagine such an evolutionary achievement. We think we are awake to reality just because our senses are working. Even if we are open to the possibility of a greater awareness, we at once despair of actually getting to it. We are subtly conditioned by modern scientific education to think of ourselves as brains, not souls, as material, not spiritual, or even mental, beings. We have been conditioned by nihilistic views that pronounce our sense of our own conscious presence to be mere illusion. And so we subliminally inhibit our spiritual growth by thinking it is merely an ineffectual illusion ending with the cessation of the brain's activity at death. So the radical evolutionary transformation required for a being to become perfectly enlightened seems impossible because of the randomness, discontinuity, and ultimate nihilism of life.

Human beings are evolving not only as physical bodies genetically interconnected through time, but also as conscious beings driven by our need to avoid suffering and our desire to achieve happiness. Within the ocean of possible forms of embodiment, the human form is already very highly developed in the pursuit of happiness, as the human body and brain have tremendous capacity to experience happiness and, conversely, are extraordinarily sensitive to pain and suffering. This extreme sensitivity to suffering is what makes humans so powerfully aggressive when frightened, and the extreme capacity for happiness is what makes us so creative in our elaboration of forms of enjoyment.

A buddha is the butterfly that finally emerges from the cocoon of the human life-form. Buddha is not just one perfected person who lived once in history. You and I will become buddhas. At least we should experiment in that direction to see what happens. We are actually incredibly close to a decisive triumph over suffering. The supreme value we give to freedom comes from our sense that the true reality is total freedom, and our knowledge of that is the doorway to our highest destiny, our supreme fulfillment.

Chapter 2

SEARCHING

FOR THE SELF

We can retrace for ourselves the steps the Buddha took by beginning where he began: with the reality of our own situation. We are highly organized socially, relatively well educated, have great technological power and industrial productivity. We have myriad forms of entertainment. The sun rises in the morning, the rains come, the water flows, the wind blows. We stay cool in summer, and warm in winter.

In the United States we live in the first country on earth with founding documents that formally guarantee the rights to life, liberty, and the pursuit of happiness. Yet we are miserable. We may blame our malaise on circumstances—our jobs, our families—or see everything around us as the source of our unhappiness. But the question arises: Will we ever find happiness from within this frame of reference? A good meal leaves us stuffed and uncomfortable. Attachment to a spouse leaves us worrying about being left alone. Pursuit of good health leads us only to the inevitability of dying. We're chasing shadows, but we see them as real, as holding the keys to our happiness.

To take responsibility for facing our living condition, we must look at who we are and how we see the world. Every day, we wake up in the morning and are hit by the biggest intuitive lie known to human consciousness. That lie goes like this: "It's me, it's me, I'm it, I'm the center of the universe. I come first. I hold it all together." The bottom line is "me." It is not just that we are selfish; it is deeper. We perceive the self as the one sure thing, the only thing, that we can count on. I am sure of my own ideas, my own dictates. I know without question what I want, what I hate, what I fear. I think, therefore I am.

I worry about myself all the time—we all do. Am I happy enough? Can I get some more? Can I get rid of that concern? Is this good for me? Is she treating me right? I am self-preoccupied, self-obsessed. Sometimes I am selfish in an obvious way; sometimes I am kind and selfless. But in either case there is no possibility of my not being self-involved.

Such self-involvement is natural, given that we see ourselves as the most important thing in the universe. Moral condemnation of it is beside the point. But I question its accuracy. While we may wake up "knowing" that we're the center of the universe, the minute we walk outside we will not encounter one single person who agrees with us. If we

could hear everyone's mind speaking out, we'd hear cho-
ruses of "It's not you, it's me! I'm the center." We are thus
in a state of constant disagreement, all in the grip of that little dictator inside telling each person that he or she is the
center of the universe.

And what does that dictator want? I want to be happy, of
course, and I work to fulfill that desire. But do I succeed in
making myself happy by merely wanting myself to be happy?
It hasn't happened yet. Operating in the grip of the obsession
of wanting myself to be happy is never successful. Maybe
the way I go about it is distorted.

When I work to make myself happy, "I" tell myself what
to do for "me." When I obey "myself," I do it unquestioningly,
as I do no other person, because I assume "I" am I. But I
seem to get little benefit from the dictates of "I." It's as
though I work for myself, but some other boss enjoys the
fruits of my efforts. I am sweating to fill up a vessel, but it
never fills. Either the water is leaking out through a hole in
the bottom, or it is being diverted into another vessel. Perhaps this "I" may not be who I really am. How could it be the
real me when it has such a distorted understanding of its
place in the universe?

How do I perceive my "I"? How do I understand myself?
When I think, "I must not allow that," "I must have this,"
where do those thoughts come from? When a friend sends a
message, "Please meet me at the pizza place at seven," I know
who sent it and I prepare to meet him. When my own inner

voice tells me, "Go for it," who do I think is sending the message?

Perhaps the answer seems self-evident: "I send myself the message." But is that true? Do we really know who that message sender is? I look for the definite thing that "I" refers to. I may thump my chest while saying "I," but I won't accept that "I" refers to my breastbone.

Am "I" my name? When someone calls my name, I respond with my entire being. But if my name is taken away, do I disappear? There is no nameplate anywhere in my physical or mental structures on which my name can land. There seems to be a point in the throat where the vowel "I" begins to sound—but that point where "I" resonates cannot be the source of my total identity. I am not my heart, my blood, my bones, my sadness, my anger, or my laughter. I am not summed up by any of my parts.

We think that the "I" is independent, static, unchanging, solid, and substantial, always the same old "me," but unique, apart from the rest of reality. Irresistible in its demands, it seems to be objective, self-evidently real, and easily identifiable. That my "I" is the core of who I am seems natural, both intuitively and objectively true. It seems to be the controller of my thoughts, the agent of my actions: When I am falsely accused, it righteously proclaims my innocence. The "I" emerges in all its glory: "I did not! I am not!" This "I" seems constantly concerned for us, but it can be completely impervious to our frailties when it is mad or desperate to possess something. It ignores our human limitations when it is obsessed with its goals. When outraged or inflamed by lust, it forces us to injure or destroy what we most dearly love, or even take our sensitive and fragile bodies and fling them at enemies with no regard for life or limb. It can push us to do things we otherwise would not think of doing. It can even order our own death. It becomes so big when we're caught in strong emotions that we can't even see it.

No matter how hard it may be for me to follow the dictates of the "I," if this "I" is who I really am, I am bound to obey. As hard as it might sometimes be for me to obey, I would have no alternative but to be what "I" am, what "I" say I must be. It would be my duty. My fate. But if I discover that I am not what "I" seem, it becomes possible that there is a real me who is other than this seemingly independent "I." In that case maybe I don't have to remain forever trapped by this bossy and impulsive "I" who claims to be seeking only my good but who constantly gets me into trouble and never seems to bring me the peace and happiness I want.

But how can I discern whether or not I am not who I am used to thinking I am? What might the real me be like? How does it look, smell, taste? How would I recognize it if I found it? To figure it out, I must look at the options of what "I" can be.

We would never embark on a major trip around the country without first checking out the vehicle. We would not just get in any old machine handed to us by someone we didn't know and take off without preparation or a map. So why are we lurching around in ideas that have been handed to us by our conditioning? Why don't we make the slightest effort to check out our identities?

Checking out the "I" is tricky. There is no consumer guide in our culture for evaluating it. The "I" seems to be a given. Its sources are not so obvious. I must try to find out who or what "I" refers to, and not accept the seemingly self-evident "I" as being undeniably real.

I am not engaging in academic philosophy. I am not saying we are nothings. I am not questioning that we are something. Doubtless I am something. I am aware that I sense myself as intrinsically a unique, self-sufficient, substantial personality mobilized by "I," referred to as "me." I am identified by "my" name, gender, race, biological status, and other stable elements of my identity, and commanded by that "I" to a certain state of existence and certain actions and experiences. What I want to find out is if I *do* actually exist in the way that I *sense* myself to exist. I want to know who is driving me, or what I am driving, before I worry about where or how to go.

Watching myself out of the corner of my mind's eye, I discover that if I pay the slightest overintensity of attention to myself, my self, puzzlingly, disappears. If I look too hard, everything I suggest to myself, everything I sift through in search of the "I"-referent, disappears under my gaze, slips right through my fingers. When the seemingly independent

"I" shifts from being the observed to being the observer, it has a hard time finding anything. So I must cultivate a subtle but dependable way of witnessing the "I" in order to assess more clearly how I habitually regard my sense of what "I" means to me.

It's like improving your tennis stroke while playing, or keeping a comfortable posture while working at a desk. You play or work with your main attention, observing and re-membering only from the side to follow through with a twist or to keep your shoulders back. When you shift focus to thinking mainly of what you are supposed to pay attention to, you lose track of the ball, you forget what's on the com-puter screen.

How can I now follow without question the dictates of this will-o'-the-wisp? How can I venture indefinitely to sus-pend judgment on this most central question of my being? I must wake up in the morning, get up, pursue the day's ac-tivities, decide what and how and when as best I can. De-termining the status of my "I" requires no less a measure of good sense.

When I am excited or in the grip of some other thought or emotion, I feel as if "I" am absolute, a prime mover, an un-deniable momentum. In order to prove to myself that I am indeed an independently existing self, I should be able to find that substantial self. If the self does exist in the way I think it should, it should not dissolve when I turn my atten-tion to it. I ask myself if the self is eluding me because I am

distracted. But if, when I put all my effort into this enterprise, I can discover no substantial self, then I will have to acknowledge the possibility that my habitual way of sensing
myself is in error. A serious search for the real self becomes
increasingly compelling.

We all start off with our habitual assumptions about ourselves in clear view, with a resolve to keep our search for this
self in a practical, commonsense context. We then bring all
our powers to bear on the search for the "I"-referent, the real
self.

We begin by looking at the body. We can again thump our
chests and say, "I'm me," but surely we are not just a bunch
of ribs. We look in the mirror and say, "There I am," but we
say the same thing when we see old snapshots of ourselves—
pictures of people whose faces were quite different then.
We disguise ourselves, we wear masks, yet there we are.
Your hand looks familiar; yet it would be you if you broke it
and it was in a cast; it would be you if you got frostbite and
your fingers were amputated. Our bodies soon crumble as
clear-cut, fixed foundations of our identities.

Let's move into more subtle dimensions and dissect ourselves mentally. We imaginatively go through the anatomy of
heart, spine, nervous system, and brain—and find no fixed
"I"-referent anywhere. We can explore cells, axons, and den-
drites; molecules, DNA, and RNA; atoms, subatomic quantum particles, unnameable forces and energies. Nowhere
can we find anything still, static, independent. Everything we
can observe or even imagine is related to something else.

We can move on to our minds and begin by sifting through our feelings, sensations, pleasures, pains, or numbnesses. When "I" seem happy, I might think I am pure pleasure; when unhappy, pure pain; when insensate, perhaps numb. Keeping close to the map of my anatomy, I investigate my sensory surfaces and, after some time, give up finding any stable, self-sufficient "I" anywhere along them.

Then we can move into images, words, symbols, ideas, concepts, mental pictures. This at first seems promising. "I" is a word, after all. The names "Alice," "Joe," "Carol," and "Shakyamuni" all are nouns. When I pronounce my own name, "Bob," does an image of myself arise in my mind? Is it a recent snapshot of my face? Is it a specification sheet? A *curriculum vitae?* A biography? Is it a favorite logo? A trademark? A symbol? None of these seems satisfactory; they all are fabrications of mine or, in the case of my name, someone else's. None touches the essence of "me." The pronouns "I" and "me" seem to *refer* to me, "myself" their *referent,* so it doesn't make sense for the word "I" *itself* to be the *real* me, to be its own referent. My solid-self-sense is triggered by my saying "I." When I repeat "me, me, me" over and over, my sense of undeniable presence is intensified, so the words bring out some referent other than themselves. But words or images alone cannot be the *real* self, since they depend on all of us agreeing on their meanings.

We can move deeper into the motions of the mind, into the emotions. When "I" love or am in love, I feel powerfully present, even in the moment of feeling that solidity melting.

When "I" hate, I am carried away by destructive impulses. When "I" feel proud, I soar above others. When "I" feel jealous, I am brought down into a nagging dislike of another. Guilt, fear, greed, confusion, even determination—all these energies seem to take hold of "me," or seem to emanate from "I." But as I think them through, observe them in actuality or in memory, they seem fully bound in relationships. As I try to trace them to their points of origin, my solid-"I"-sense detects the elusive presence of the real "I" or "me" there, but I cannot seem to follow the thread of energy to that source. If a feeling were like a rope tied to a post, I could follow it along and then grab the post. But it's not—as I near the sensed locus of "I," it again seems to trail off and evaporate. And, in fact, a post is not independent but completely relative and bound up in relations: It is stuck in the ground; the rope is attached to a part of it; too much pressure will pull it over; and so forth. Likewise, a solid-"I"-referent could not in principle be any sort of final point of connection. How could thoughts and feelings be connected to it, if it stands solidly self-sufficient, not connected to anything?

At last we come to awareness itself, to looking at our very consciousness. This can be strenuous, because we must direct our consciousness to look for itself while being itself. Luckily, some aspects of consciousness are not remote. We are conscious of what we see, for example; a visual consciousness seems to mirror what our eyes perceive out there. As our eyes move around from object to object, we recognize table, finger, page, word, blue, sky, and mountain in the distance. Our consciousness seems to change as its contents change. Sometimes it is aware of just light and color, without recognizing anything. The act of recognition requires another consciousness bringing out an idea or remembered image and matching it with what we are seeing. Then we can sift through our other sensory consciousnesses, noticing clearly what we usually let slide into the background. Our auditory consciousness is endlessly stimulated by trucks, crows, the washing machine, voices, and sometimes a humming in our ears that seems to come from nowhere outside. We turn to olfactory consciousness, which we often do not notice unless we run into a bad smell, like an industrial smell, or a good smell, like perfume. We move to taste, which we usually focus on just when we eat. Finally we get to tactile consciousness, which constantly gives us information though we focus on it most strongly during sexual activity.

Taking our time, we sort through all these consciousnesses, remembering their vast variety. In the end we have to acknowledge that we cannot find anything at their cores that seems unitary, stable, or independent, though we still sense the solid self behind them all, most vivid in our memories being responses of love and hate.

When we examine our senses more deeply, we become increasingly aware of how smoothly our focus moves from one sense-consciousness to another. We now inhale a sweet fragrance; we now listen for a familiar tune; we now notice the texture of our leather armrest. That ability, we discover, lies in our sense of an inner arena—an inner theater of awareness—the area where we see our inner images, where we watch the videos of memory. Where is that theater within us? We often think of the images as dancing through our brains.

Try this experiment. Picture a coin, a quarter with George Washington's head on it. Where does its image land? At first it seems to be in your head, on a screen somewhere behind your eyes. It is hard to hold it stable, so let it rotate around in your mind's eye until you see it sideways, and then let it flip over to the eagle side. Envision it in your throat, then in the center of your torso, at solar plexus level up against your spine. Next, visualize it at the base of the spine, and move it down your leg to your knee or foot. We can visualize this quarter, always fleetingly, wherever we decide to see it. So we can imagine the inner awareness monitor, the movie screen, functioning wherever we want, not only in the head.

We notice that we also mobilize a virtual imagining process when we dream. In dreams, we see things, we hear things, yet our eyes and ears are closed to waking awareness. With what eyes did I see the Eiffel Tower in last night's dream of Paris? There must be a subtle area of consciousness that can function without being attached to the five senses and the consciousness bound up in their operations. To get to the bottom of this mystery of the solid-"I"-sense, we have to investigate this most subtle working of consciousness, this "mental consciousness."

When we look at it carefully, we find that mental consciousness parallels the five senses we have in our waking consciousness. Usually it coordinates with the sense consciousnesses, pays attention to sense-objects, recognizes them, reacts to them, selects among them. With a little more effort, we note that it can function also in a realm of pure imagery, calling up picture after picture and reviewing them in its inner eye. It can also listen to inner voices: When you think to yourself, you hear words in your inner voice. You can even see the words move on an inner screen while you hear the voice pronounce them if you want to.

Now, if there is indeed a solid "I," if it is my real self, it must be the final register of all my impressions, the actual agency of knowing them, the Central Processing Unit. I try to focus on that, but I become a little dizzy as I begin to chase after a glimpse of my own awareness. I try to turn back from the inner monitor and inner speaker to the inner observer who looks and listens. But to turn toward my center of awareness, I have to tell my awareness to turn back on itself; it's like whirling my body as a dervish does, spinning to catch sight of the tip of my nose as my eye flies past where my nose just was. I'm looking for the little creature inside who is running the show.

Right away this little-homunculus imagery falls apart. If

there is another miniature me-body in a chamber looking out a window, it has eyes, an inner observer, an identity; it is changing; it is bound up in relationships, perceptions, thoughts, awarenesses; it would have to have another little homunculus within its chamber looking out its window into the inner monitor, and speakers with its own inner register. The image simply transposes into ever more microdimensions, dissolving through an infinitely diminishing microscopic tunnel.

Pressing on to find our own awareness, we turn and we turn around the sensed axis, pushing to get ever closer to the axis itself, finding the limits of inner eyes and ears, monitors and speakers. The sensed axis around which we chase our awareness disappears as we try to close in on it, bringing to us a subtle inner dizziness that can be frightening and even nauseating as it becomes more intense. One has to make a kind of supreme effort to persist through this. The inner voice, now perhaps shouting, now sounding alienated and afraid, calls us to stop. If we have carefully worked up to this moment, the voice might also reassure us not to worry. If the self is a solid core, it is absolute and self-sufficient and cannot be destroyed by our search—we are dizzy only from the unaccustomed effort of trying to see it as it is. We begin to perceive the illusion of solidity and come close to discovering what we really are.

The dizziness heralds our initial glimpse of the dissolution of the self as solid. When we recognize that the dizziness also is not solid, we let go of it and feel as if we were dissolving, becoming a voidness melting in a voidness. We can reassure ourselves that any voidness is not solid, but at the same time it is not nothing and cannot obstruct our awareness. Even a dark void is something, so any sense of falling into nothing is but our own conjuring of voidness. The minute we let go of either attraction or resistance to the feeling of dissolving, it stops being frightening and turns into a pleasant feeling of floating freely. We lose all sense of boundary, all tension of struggle, and experience a vast, sky-like feeling of endless, all-inclusive realness, a realness that gently and unobtrusively seems to be connected to all other beings and things. This is the real self, an inexhaustible well of peace and happiness, incorporating all, fulfilling all desires, embracing all others without neglecting ourselves. This is the essence of what the Buddha saw during his own meditation.

It is the experience we've been looking for, the perfect relief from our uncertainty about the self, the complete release from a habitual sense of isolation and self-enclosure. Feeling intimately connected to the entire universe, feeling it all as your very body, you break free from all fear, joyfully and inconceivably overwhelmed by the bliss of release, swimming in a sense of an absolute melting into utter relativity.

It is difficult to capture this experience in words, though words are important in helping us cut loose from our habitual alienation. All solid-time-sense drops away at this event-horizon, and so there is no clearly defined "moment" of our disappearing into that utter relativity. (We can learn a little lesson about our ingrained escapism when we feel a shudder of disappointment at *not* being obliterated by some imagined final reality.) We could say also that since the moment of our disappearance has no definable length, it does not obstruct our instantaneous reappearance. But now our constant, instantaneous disappearance and reappearance—our infinite transparency—imparts a new vividness and clarity to the infinite network of the relatedness of things and beings. All things and beings now appear as if on the endlessly convoluted surface of the shining mirror of their diffused absoluteness. It seems paradoxical that having decisively dissolved our absolute, independent sense of self we should now be so aware of the essence of each and every thing. Our habitual solidity-sense has become transparent, and things' objectivity no longer hides any apparent intrinsic self-sufficiency, nor does it reflect any intrinsic self-sufficient subjectivity. Everything seems dreamlike and illusory, yet things seem present in a way no longer separate from their dissolution. Our solidity-sense is blissfully dissolved while creatively present; our self-sense is simultaneously in union with others.

This is not a mystical or mysterious state. It is a matter of commonsense recognition. When we see a car behind us in the rearview mirror, it looks like it is actually coming at us head-on, that the steering wheel is on the right and that it will pass us on the right. Our knowledge of the mirror's left/right distortion automatically corrects, and we hold steady to let the car go by us on the left. This is not a mystical achievement. So now, when I feel "I" as self-sufficiently, imperiously solid, I deal with its dictates, channel its impulses, and participate in its thoughts, while my experiential knowledge of its lack of solidity automatically corrects for it and works with it as a relative process within the inconceivable network of dependencies.

Far from dwelling in some sort of mystical state of disappearance, I am now at home in reality, free of ordinary states of alienation wherein things seem as if some inscrutable depth of absoluteness lay behind them. At last I am immune to any temptation to mystify some extraordinary state of dissolution, some absolute nothingness or absolute beingness, and make it the goal of my existence. I now know all these absolutes as precisely one with all relationalities, which for the first time emerge in all their translucent vividness as the focus of all concern.

Out of the wisdom of natural freedom from any intrinsically solid self comes an inexhaustible compassion for all life—including for myself. Concern for the greatest well-being of all relative things, their happiness or freedom from suffering, becomes my absolute concern because of their utter relatedness to me.

This primary exercise, or yoga, is a way to begin to transform the self-preoccupation that causes chronic suffering
into the insightful, gradual opening and letting go of the self
that is paradoxically self-fulfilling—I become an ever-
happier being in my unconcern for my self. This process is
long and gradual, though there are powerful methods for
accelerating it once one has embarked.

There have been millions of persons who have awakened
to their true reality, who have been called "enlightened" in
many civilizations. They have not seen the universe only
the way we moderns are taught to see it—as a vast, dark,
freezing void through which galaxies are scattered, very few
having stars with planets bathed in a green-blue film of oxy-
gen and carbon and perhaps just one planet supporting sentient life as we know it. Ours is an impossibly paranoid,
lonely, isolated vision. No wonder we feel weird. We conceive our living to be such a rare exception, so fragile, so
meaningless.

The truly alive see an infinitude of universes, a beginningless, boundless sea of life, energy, and delight, full of
goodness, aware of itself in its absolute ultimate peace and
security, freedom and happiness. They see us, even as we
struggle to stay separate, as totally incorporated within that
sea of joy, nothing neglected, no one excluded. They feel
one with us completely, just as we are. And they experience
our individual feelings of confusion, loneliness, and terror.
They see precisely how we have closed off our own deeper

sense of union with the sea of all goodness. They call this habitual misperception our "ignorance," our "misknowledge."

We look through the Hubble telescope, we have walked
in space, we know it's dark and cold out there. Some of us
figure statistically there must be life on other planets, but still
we have not yet physically found another planet that can support life. Have these "enlightened" people fallen into a psy-
chotic delusion, hallucinating lights in the darkness, warmth
in the cold, life in dead stone? Perhaps. But when you put on
the Army's latest night-vision infrared combat glasses, you
can see things in what looks to your naked eye to be pitch
darkness. Solar panels extract heat from light rays in freezing space. Radio signals activate receivers in silent space.
Space and atoms are energies, forces—gravitational, elec-
tromagnetic, weak, and strong. What if enlightened people
see on the extremely subtle level of the quantum forces?
What if they experience the strong force directly as the energy of life? What if they naturally identify with limitless
space as a live body? Our dark space may look to them like
a sea of light. Our solid bodies may seem diaphanous, holo-
graphic arrangements of infinite space to them. How can we
insist, after learning that the atoms making up our bodies are
mostly space—each a Yankee Stadium whose "matter" is a
nucleus the size of a golf ball on home plate, its electrons
buzzing like flies in the bleachers—that our habitual sense-
perception of outer space as cold, dark, and dead is a revelation of the one and only reality of space?

Religious people, west and east, have always tended to feel there is a mysterious power of life in everything. The appearance of darkness and pain and death is overcome by a glorious light of goodness in most forms of religion. What Jews, Christians, Muslims, and Hindus call "God," or perhaps "Godhead," is a force of reality much like the infinite ocean-body of living joy that great Buddhist meditators experience. When a believer asserts unshakable faith in the face of the worst experience or apparent reality, she or he is reaching for connection to the deepest awareness of infinite living energy. Enlightened people do not see this boundlessness as something other than themselves. They experience themselves as one with all gods and all other beings. They consider us all capable of becoming fully aware of our own freedom and happiness. Faith in such a possibility is a good place to begin this journey to liberation; it encourages us to set forth. But we all can move beyond faith to direct experience and full knowledge of our true state.

Whether or not enlightenment is a plausible goal for us is a vital question for our lives. If it is possible for us to attain such perfect enlightenment ourselves, our whole sense of meaning and our place in the universe immediately changes. To be open to this possibility is to be a spiritual seeker, no matter what our religion. Enlightenment is not meant to be an object of religious faith. It is an evolutionary goal, something we want to become, like president of the United States, a concert violinist, or a great poet. Once we recognize the biological possibility of our evolving into be-ings of full understanding, we can begin to imagine ourselves as buddhas, awakened or enlightened beings.

"Buddha" is not a personal name. It is a title, a state we can attain. It means "awakened," "blossomed," "enlightened." It is the blossoming of all happiness and positive powers. By def-inition, being enlightened is a fully evolved way of living. It is perfect freedom—a freedom so total it cannot be lost even in relationships. It is perfect security, certain of its re-ality, perfection, and eternal bliss—it is the goal in the quest for happiness.

This evolutionary process and its result of buddhahood have profound effects on the individual, on the society one is a member of, and, by resonance, on the whole world. These effects are incalculable by our usual yardsticks of self- and social improvement, being a transformation of the very ground of the social contract. A society of enlightened beings is bound to be an enlightened society.

Chapter 3

THE COOL
REVOLUTION

*P*atrick Henry's famous cry, "Give me liberty or give me death!" was a political statement. We must understand this statement as both scientific and spiritual. We must taste liberty as that thing we most want. We must make freedom a reality on the living, biological, and evolutionary levels, not only an ideal. Only then can we know what we are saying when we say "give me liberty." Without knowing the taste of freedom, "give me death" is a pretense, a bluff easily called. When threatened with death, we beg for the safety of bondage in exchange for our lives. Our modern politics of enlightenment tries to help us with our lives, our liberties, and our pursuits of happiness. If we are free politically but not free of our unhappiness, how much liberty do we really have? If we make the effort to understand what life, liberty, and happiness are in the context of the work of enlightenment, then we can become real participants in the politics that aims for those goals.

Buddha's vision was for an entirely new kind of civilization, one based on the assumption of the possibility of enlightenment for all citizens. He placed the highest value on
individual freedom, since individual development is the highest purpose of the entire society. As the individuals evolve toward buddhahood, so does the society evolve toward a
buddhaland. It is a process that has been unfolding since the
fifth century B.C.E., and we can see the roots the Buddha
put down sprouting in our own time.

"Politics," as its derivation from the Greek *polis* (city) indicates, is a general term that covers not all human interactions but particularly those interactions among equals who
are focused on the concern for self-government. Politics first
occurred in our historical cycle when the restless militant
tribes of the Eurasian continent learned the ways of the
river-valley civilizations. Those civilizations had developed an
agricultural surplus, adapted to confinement in cities, and
come to see that rational norms of interaction could be established between tribes and that discourse could take place
without sharing the same ritual matrix, language, or lineage.
Politics is a middle way between battle and ritual.

The rise of politics was part of the same enlightening milieu that supported the rise of teachers such as Socrates and
the Buddha. This development occurred simultaneously in
Greece, Egypt, Mesopotamia, Iran, China, and India. In the
Greek city-states, Socrates had a number of colleagues and
predecessors. Confucius managed to live a full life span, trav-

eling among the city-states of late Chou dynasty China. In India, Shakyamuni wandered among the city-states of the Ganges River plain and the other minor republican towns to the north, along with flocks of ascetics, sages, emancipated peasants, and educated women. It was in India also that the critical space between battle and ritual was most broadly opened—thousands of liberal academies would flourish uninterruptedly for the next 1,500 years. But in the larger context, this enlightening milieu was situated in the early stages of the cycles of wars over territories held by the city-states that eventually became the clashes of nations, empires, and superpowers that continue even now.

Buddha abandoned all sides of the many conflicts of the day, his royal privilege, and became a mendicant. He entered a spiritual family, leaving behind his racial and national identity. He became propertyless, abandoning the competition for wealth and ownership. He became viewless, abandoning all ideological identity and all dogmatism. He became selfless, abandoning all personal clamor for recognition. He even let go of life, abandoning all violent claims to air, food, water, and other valuable resources. Thus abandoning all ordinary roles, he created a new role: that of the person who lives *in* the world but not *of* the world, who connects himself and therefore others to a transcendent reality that puts the demands of relative reality into the context of transcendence.

Radical individualism, which makes the individual's need

to attain full development the highest good, is the key to preserving the openness necessary for a truly political society. For individualism to flourish, it requires an economic surplus, and India had the greatest wealth of the ancient world. It needs some form of education that encourages the development of critical thinking, and a social matrix that extends support to nonconformity. These conditions had just become possible in India in Buddha's time, and his activities can be understood as gently contributing to them.

Siddhartha left his throne to seek a precise understanding of reality in order to serve society better. After experiencing that comprehensive awareness which he called awakening or enlightenment, he did not float away on a cloud of bliss into some otherworldly realm. He stood up and began a sustained campaign of social action, offering all people in all nations a chance to improve their moral, emotional, and intellectual lives, while creating a greater world for future generations. By founding institutions of education, he initiated, on the cultural and social levels, a politics of enlightenment.

The Western Enlightenment of the seventeenth and eighteenth centuries had an obvious social impact. From its faith in reason and critique of traditional ideas came the revolutionary movements espousing liberty, equality, fraternity—the ideals of democracy. Such revolutions were innovations in a Western history of unfair monarchs and tyrants. The Buddha's enlightenment, however, had a social dimension that is harder for us to see. His movement was not the founding of a religion—it was the founding of a new educational system, a cultural and social revolution that consciously avoided taking over the existing institutions of government.

A revolution that transforms the outlook and behavior of many individuals and thereby slowly transforms a society can be called a "cool" revolution. It educates people to think critically, to enter that realm of nonconformity that has always been the source of change. When people have transformed their minds, they will naturally and coolly act to transform the society and eventually the polity. Shakyamuni turned politics on its head and proved that the best way to build a healthy society was from the bottom up—through the development of the individual—not from the top down.

The Buddha's core insight of the lack of static identity of any person or thing exploded the root notions of social conditioning. When we understand the lack of fixed selves as the bases of the various conventional identities—priest, warrior, merchant, laborer, outcast, man, woman, native, alien, white, black—their nonabsoluteness is rendered plainly and the tendency to rigidity or fanaticism is greatly reduced. The unbound self, having seen through socially imposed role-playing, gains the intellectual freedom to begin to evolve his or her own identity.

In the Buddha's time, the law of karmic evolution became a powerful support for individualism. According to that theory, all things come about because of myriad causes and conditions, and everything that happens leads to further effects for individuals. The only way to break the cycle is to eliminate the negative effects and cultivate only the positive. The Buddha's genius turned this scientific philosophy into an empirical one of the evolutionary effects of individual action. It thus became the basis of the fundamental laws of moral behavior, the Buddhist "ten commandments": not to kill, steal, misbehave sexually, lie, slander, abuse, chatter, covet, hate, and hold false views. Or, put positively, to save lives; give gifts; behave well sexually; tell the truth; speak reconcilingly, pleasantly, and meaningfully; be detached; love unconditionally; and hold authentic views. The ethical alternatives—choosing between giving and stealing, between truth and lies, between love and hate—were seen to be the pathways to evolutionary advancement or degeneration.

These innovations drove the Buddha's political strategy. He shocked contemporaries by accepting as disciples individuals from all walks of life, women as well as men, monastics and laypeople, cutting across caste boundaries. He taught people not to rely on traditional authority but to use their critical reason to figure out the nature of reality. He created the institution of monasticism for his community of mendicants by getting all members of the society to acknowledge that individuals should be free to pursue their own liberation without being constrained by duties to family, village, tribe, or state, and without regard for class or sex, thereby winning for his students and successors the precious social space to carry on their practices of self-cultivation. These actions all were major social breakthroughs.

The importance of this historical innovation of monasticism should not be underestimated. In the code for the new monastic order, Shakyamuni took pains to ensure that the mendicants should not become another order of priests: He forbade them to officiate at birth, marriage, or death ceremonies; to touch money, own property, and so forth; to perform any service to society. They were not to justify their existence in any way. And yet they were to live near the towns and cities, they were to enter the streets each morning to beg for food and share their insights. On the foundation of a permanent free lunch, the monastic community stood as an unmistakable reminder that society exists to serve the individual, to create space for his or her liberation from ignorance.

What the Buddha did as a revolutionary was to shift the social ethos from collectivism to individualism; to redefine the highest good as transcendent liberation, not mundane success; to replace the competitive struggle of egocentric identities with a cooperative interaction of eccentric individuals. He worked to transform violence into nonviolence, greed into generosity, self-indulgence into sensitivity, deceitfulness into honesty, and, most important, ignorance into insight. To succeed, he needed a vast educational institution which had to be funded on a long-term basis and had to be able to spread widely from state to state without being perceived as a threat by the social and religious authorities. The order of monks and nuns was designed to achieve these ends.

In the process of unleashing monasticism as a mechanism for transforming society, Shakyamuni also demythologized the monarchy, replacing domination with generosity as the primary quality required of a king. He encouraged the merchant class—who converted the individual virtue of generosity into the world-transforming engine of commerce—to supplant the warriors as the major providers of society, thereby beginning the shift from warfare to trade that we still have not fully completed today. He explicitly delineated the boundaries of royal power, stressing the karmic accountability of a king for his actions. He was not impressed by the monarchs of his time, though he did not shrink from them either, counseling and teaching them as he did everyone else.

The experience of selflessness as freedom from alienated ego-addiction is a revolution in the deepest heart of the individual. It is a turn from pained and fearful self-centeredness to joyful, loving relatedness. This inner experience is the indispensable pivot of the cool revolution that Buddha started in order to gradually transform world civilization over the last 2,500 years.

Shakyamuni's first act was his choice of strategy. He could have chosen any number of paths of action. The most obvious one would have been to return to his own throne and run his country on enlightened principles. Had Shakyamuni become a world emperor, he could have implemented, at least throughout the Indian subcontinent, a golden era of prosperity, harmony, universal education, and liberation. How can it be that he benefited the planet more as a buddha? The Buddha's strategy was a pedagogical necessity. Under a buddha who chose to teach from an emperor's throne, people would obey the enlightenment laws of nonviolence and so forth because of the coercive influence of fear of the imperial power. They would follow the path of basic virtuous conduct. But the higher virtues, the mental and spiritual virtues needed to achieve positive karmic evolution—generosity, love, tolerance, and penetrating wisdom—cannot be fulfilled by mere obedience to laws. To understand the nature of reality, one has to explore reality through an arduous and voluntary internal effort and break through the habits and preconceptions of ignorance. Enlightenment education cannot work as indoctrination by means of authoritative commands: "Open your mind!" "Accept selflessness!"

The self has to be given the free space to turn around in its habitual tracks and observe itself in a new way. Enlightenment teaching must be a noncoercive provision of guidance for self-emergence. The wisdom to realize selflessness, to find the endlessly loving heart toward others, to find the strength for tolerance, has its source within the individual. If the Buddha had returned to his throne to spread the teaching, the new truth would have become identified with the Shakya nation locally, with the Indian empire on the world scale, and with the Shakya age in the historical record. It would have had a great impact, no doubt, but it never could have spread throughout all humanity and all history, emerging from the depths of people's hearts.

Buddha was not the founder of a religion—he discovered no omnipotent God who charged him to move the masses, and he saw that converting people to a new belief would not bring them any nearer to freedom. Buddha was not a revolutionary leader in that he held no wrath against the kings of his day. He understood that what was needed was not merely the changing of beliefs or the holders of power but the changing of the entire culture's perception of reality, power, life, and death. His was a middle way between prophet and revolutionary; his role best described as teacher, educator of people's understanding and goodwill. He is sometimes called *Jina,* "victor," since he conquered the self by understanding the truth and thereby gained the ability to bring others to the same victory over themselves.

The monastic social movement that emerged from the Axial Age in India swept throughout Asia, transforming the landscapes, the cultures, and the politics of all its nations, as well as countless individuals. It is quite likely that it influenced even West Asia, North Africa, and Europe by lending its institutional style to Aramaic and Egyptian Christianity as well as to Manicheanism.

Monasticism was designed to embody, in an alternative social reality, the seeds of the planetary buddhaland, which the Buddha saw would emerge in the future. Monasticism was the center of what he called the "Jewel Community," a specially protected community within society that enabled individuals to develop an extraordinary standard of ethical, religious, and intellectual life oriented to transcendent individual and social fulfillment. Indian society already had the institutions of the hermit ascetic and the priesthood of the urban temple. In between these two, the Buddha gradually evolved the institutional form of the suburban monastery, just adjacent to and still virtually within the existing social world.

The boundary between his community and the ordinary society was a change of identity so drastic that it involved a psychic death and rebirth. The monk or nun had to abandon race, caste, family, name, property, occupation, clothing, adornment, hair, even sexuality. The seriousness of this boundary was essential to insulate the monastic heart of the new community from the powerful demands of the larger social whole.

In the new community of monks and nuns, the members could cultivate a new way of relating to one another—without violence, exploitation, or competitive roughness. Because each was seeking transcendent liberation, there was a new consideration for the individual; a new sensitivity toward others as ends in themselves; a new respect for freedom, personal attainment, and wisdom. They put the Buddha's psychological methods of self-cultivation into practice to free themselves from debilitating negative passions and to enjoy the happiness of the positive emotions. All of them, including women and members of the lower castes, could study the penetrating philosophical teachings of the Buddha. They could critique the conventional notions of the culture and attain liberative and transformative insight into the nature of the self and reality. Thus, the new community served as an ethical proving ground for a future buddhaland society, as psychological asylum and meditative retreat, as philosophical school, research laboratory, and cultural center.

The monastic community also served a number of mediating functions that were incidental to its main ones but that probably were important for its rapid and successful expansion throughout northern India. Its openness to women, to people of low caste, and to ex-slaves made it an important avenue of social mobility as well as a mechanism of social cohesion. It is perhaps for this reason that the rising mercantile classes of Indian society, some of whom came from the lower rungs of the traditional hierarchy and from the outsider castes, found their needs and aspirations satisfied by the monastic community and were its most important and enthusiastic backers.

This new institution was fundamentally the footing, the

grounding point, for the Buddha's vision of an enlightened society, which would spread across the planet gradually through history. It became a fountain of goodness through systematic restraint of evil; a haven of peace through concentration of mind and cultivation of positive emotion; and a center of learning, understanding, and knowledge through systematic inquiry into the true nature of reality. Monasticism institutionalized the primacy of the individual's life-purpose of enlightenment over the collective's purposes of survival and production.

As a cool-war general, the Buddha sent out his army of monks and nuns to infiltrate all countries. Within two centuries, the north of India had merged into a single empire, and in a parallel, invisible, and purely interior process, the Buddha's community and its schools had become a widespread establishment, referred to simply as "the community."

The social miracle Buddha performed was to get the kings of his day to accept the intrusion of this vast, materially purposeless institution. At that time, the kings of the sixteen main states of northern India were vying with one another for imperial domination, and yet most of them supported the community. None of the other great reformers of his era—not Socrates, Confucius, Isaiah, or Zoroaster—was able to win the support of their rulers to establish a powerful school, much less an international community. The kings' acceptance of the Buddha and his monastic movement marked the birth of functioning radical individualism in Indian civilization.

When monasticism flourishes, large numbers of young potential soldiers tend to seek salvation rather than serve their country, so it would seem reasonable to think that the royal class would be opposed to it. Although individual monks renounce property, the pious take pleasure in donating lands and treasures to the monasteries, and soon substantial landholdings and revenues go off the royal tax rolls. A significant part of the labor force can become tied up in "otherworldly" pursuits and diminish the ranks of farmers, artisans, and other sorts of producers.

For Buddhist monasticism to have flourished so strongly in Buddha's India, these obvious drawbacks to monasticism from the royal perspective must not have been decisive. There must have been a surplus of recruits, land, and treasure. It must have provided a safety valve of liberationist energies, perhaps safer for the polity than having idle malcontents. It must have been the religious wave among the merchants who financed royal adventures. It must have provided a special meaning to the kings themselves so that they could see their reigns as leaving behind something generous and useful.

Those kings who supported Buddhism did not have to give up all their mundane ambitions. On the contrary, they perceived the community and its charismatic leadership to be assets to their reigns, as conferring distinctly this-worldly blessings upon them in exchange for their support. King Ajatashatru of Magadha, at one time an enemy of Shakyamuni, sent his minister to the Buddha for counsel on his invasion plans of a neighboring republic during the very days the Buddha was preparing to die. And it was the Magadhan kings, the foremost supporters of the community, who eventually won the imperial title.

Militarism and monasticism are connected in that they are mirror opposites of each other. Shakyamuni himself had been trained in all the royal arts, including the art of pulling together and deploying an army. His was an antiarmy seeking to conquer the world of ignorance and fear. Until it went underground during the invasions that overwhelmed India at the end of the first millennium, his army culturally and spiritually conquered most of Asia. What happened to it later is a subtle question, precisely because of Buddha's nonviolent reaction to violent opposition. The community's response to persecution often took unexpected forms.

The phenomenal success of monasticism, eventually Eurasia-wide, can be understood as the progressive truth-conquest of the world. The Buddha designed his life, teachings, and institutions to permeate all human societies, bringing with them the individual calm, self-control, intelligence, and goodwill that is the heart of civilization. Many people attained freedom during the Buddha's lifetime—his teaching and community spread widely throughout India without forceful imposition or evangelism.

Since then, the human community has grown ever more powerful in spite of its recurring habit of destructive violence that has brought it again and again to the brink of extinction. It is clearer than ever that the value of self-conquest through self-transcendence, of violence-conquest through nonviolence, is not at all unrealistic idealism but indispensable to life itself. If the planet survives, as the buddhas long ago declared that it would, then the triumph of civilization as truth-conquest will be complete, human beings will at last have tamed their hatred and violence, and the buddha-land will be openly manifest.

Chapter 4

A KINGLY
REVOLUTION

*D*uring the two centuries after the Buddha's passing away, the descendants of his friend King Bimbisara of Magadha gradually conquered the fifteen other city-states of northern India and established an empire. This empire soon was challenged unsuccessfully by Alexander the Great, only to be taken over from within by Chandragupta Maurya, who had been a general in the service of the last Magadhan king.

His grandson Ashoka became Maurya emperor around 262 B.C.E., ruling over northern India. One of his first acts was to invade the neighboring kingdom of Kalinga and annex its territories. As he rode home across the battlefield, he was deeply moved by the carnage. He heard widows weeping and saw children wandering among the corpses. He began to wonder if conquering a people was worth it, if the negative moral and emotional consequences of the destruction and oppression were not greater than the benefits of dominion over a ruined people. He became repentant about the violence of his conquest by the sword and, remembering who had long ago condemned it, had an insight that there was a consciousness higher than his own, some reality transcendent even to his imperial will. Ashoka turned to the Buddha's teachings and commemorated his change of heart by erecting giant pillars and carving edicts into rock all around his empire. The edicts are a remarkable record of his principles and policies, and of his aspirations for himself and his people. The famous Rock Edict XIII invites us to meet Ashoka and touch the mind of this extraordinary person.

The Kalinga country was conquered by King Ashoka in the eighth year of his reign. One hundred fifty thousand persons were carried away captive, 100,000 were slain, and many times that number died. Immediately after the Kalingas had been conquered, King Ashoka became intensely devoted to the study of truth, to the love of truth, and to the understanding of truth. King Ashoka, conqueror of the Kalingas, is moved to remorse now. For he has felt profound sorrow and regret because the conquest of a people previously unconquered involved slaughter, death, and deportation.*

---

*This and the following translations are from Nikam and McKeown, *The Edicts of Aśoka* (Chicago: University of Chicago Press, 1974).

Ashoka's ability to see the folly of his ways, feel remorse, adopt an alternative, and publicly admit his error is all too rare among wielders of power, especially a ruler at the height of his power and not under any pressure to change. After confessing his remorse, Ashoka revealed his newly espoused values, asserting the purpose of human life to be liberation through realization of truth by means of the sincere practice of any faith. He declared that neither Brahmins nor Buddhists should be destroyed by war. His endorsement of the Buddhist cool revolution from hatred and fighting into compassion and nonviolence was thoroughgoing, and under his rule, the countercultural, revolutionary Buddhist movement was granted an officially sanctioned role as an educational and religious institution close to the heart of the national purpose. Ashoka's transformed imperialism became a benevolent imperialism of Dharma.

> King Ashoka considers truth-conquest the most important conquest. He has achieved this truth-conquest repeatedly both here and among the people living beyond the borders of his kingdom, even as far away as 3,000 miles, where Antiochus II Theos of Syria (261–246 B.C.E.) rules, and even beyond Antiochus in the realms of the four kings named Ptolemy II Philadelphos (285–247 B.C.E.), Antigonos Gonatos of Macedonia (278–239 B.C.E.), Magas of Cyrene (300–258 B.C.E.), and Alexander of Epirus (272–258 B.C.E.), and to the south . . . as far as Sri Lanka. Here in the

king's dominion also . . . everywhere people heed his instructions in truth. Even in countries which King Ashoka's envoys have not reached, people have heard about truth and about His Majesty's ordinances and instructions in truth, and they themselves conform to truth and will continue to do so.

Ashoka presented his spiritual revolution from the top down as a campaign of conquest, contrasting his new campaign of truth-conquest with the old campaign of sword-conquest. By "truth-conquest," Ashoka was referring specifically to the program launched by Shakyamuni Buddha, "truth" (Dharma) meaning the Buddha's teaching, the reality of freedom at its core, and the path to that freedom, and "conquest" meaning sending a few unarmed monks out with caravans to spread the teachings of enlightenment to all the kingdoms of the rest of Asia.

The Buddha's cool revolution operated through the creation of an alternative social realm, an educational community within but insulated against the ordinary society, where the individual's purpose in life could be focused intently on the attainment and communication of enlightenment. "Dharma" was previously defined as "religion"—the binding structuring of belief and duty, of obligations and law—the structure of authority. So Buddha's redefining Dharma as a truth that liberated people from all of these binding structures was powerfully revolutionary. His revolution was cool, not a hot war, because it created a new sphere of liberty alongside the social sphere of bondage. It made no attempt to change the existing mores by force, but rather in the most unintrusive, unthreatening way, through the spread of teachings anchored in monastic practices.

When Ashoka adopted the campaign several centuries later, the cool revolution had come a long way, and the two meanings of Dharma—the old religious law and the new implications of freedom—gave Ashoka's edicts a fertile ambiguity. Ashoka became the agent of heating up the cool revolution, imposing its truth by royal action and authority, but he did not mount any sort of religious war. He built many monuments, expanded educational institutions, moderated the workings of the justice system, extended the welfare functions of the state, and made the enlightenment ideal prominent in all aspects of the people's lives. Thus did the cool revolution rise to the level of establishment power, with mixed results. Although these changes had enormous impacts on the physical and cultural infrastructures of Indian civilization, by heating up the revolution, Ashoka got ahead of the evolutionary level of the people and stirred up resistance from various elite sectors, from traditional religious groups, and even from his own family. In fact, the idealistic standard he set shortened the duration of his empire. But Ashoka himself firmly believed that his truth-conquest was at least far better than his previous policy of violence.

Wherever conquest is achieved by truth, it produces satisfaction. Satisfaction is firmly established by truth-conquest.
Even satisfaction, however, is of little importance. King
Ashoka attaches value ultimately only to consequences of action in the future life. This edict on truth has been inscribed
so that my children and great-grandchildren who may come
after me should not think new conquests worth achieving.
If they do conquer, let them take pleasure in moderation and
mild punishments. Let them consider truth-conquest the
only true conquest. This is good, here and hereafter. Let
their pleasure be pleasure in truth. For this alone is good,
here and hereafter.

While he transformed society, Ashoka did not entirely
succeed in transforming his own habits to fit the Buddhist
mold. He remained quite hot-tempered, could sometimes
react violently, enjoyed his royal power in a way that left no
doubt that he would not have made a good monk. But he invested all his competitive spirit and his imperial taste for
fame and grandeur in his work of patronage of the Dharma.
He wanted to give more to enlightenment and its tradition
than any king ever had given or ever could give in history.

Ashoka's change is an instance of power not corrupting
but leading to improvement. He had been demented in his
quest to dominate the world around him, but once he succeeded in his original ambition, he saw the hollowness of
his worldly victory. His conversion is not believed by some

modern historians. They argue that it was a show of piety on the part of a cynical, unscrupulous ruler, intended to aggrandize himself and disarm any rivals. Those who argue this way are defending a notion of politics as a quintessentially secular enterprise, divorced from morality and spiritual ideas, based on strictly utilitarian considerations. Thus, any instance of power being wielded benevolently is *a priori* suspect, as counterevidence to the theory. The Buddhist view is that Ashoka's conversion was purely a ripening of positive evolution, an awakening of a humanistic instinct within the fighter's heart.

To reconcile this contradiction, one has to understand how both are right yet neither is the whole picture. Ashoka was genuinely converted in the sense that he saw the practical superiority of moral and enlightened policy. Conveniently, his conversion served the interests of the state, since an empire at its maximum coherent state of expansion is better controlled by an internal, peaceful ethic of self-restraint than by expensive, potentially rebellious, militaristic police forces. The *Arthashastra,* a work in political economy more ruthless, subtle, and pragmatic than anything Machiavelli could have dreamed up, was written by a minister of Ashoka's grandfather, the king who had defeated Alexander the Great. It exemplified the main Indian tradition of political science at this time, a totally utilitarian, amoral, ruthless pursuit of power and wealth. In this work, much thought is given to the problem of demilitarizing a warrior elite after a campaign requiring their services has concluded. If they are not provided for in a proper manner, they may revolt against the ruler. A careful formula is presented: Settle the most dangerous the farthest away; send in agents to forestall conspiracies by creating divisive caste taboos; and encourage new channels for the retired warriors' energies.

But the *Arthashastra* does not provide any method for reeducating the warrior to develop an internalized ethic of loyalty and peacefulness. Ashoka had to look to Buddhism and other Indian ascetic traditions such as Jainism for assistance in this enterprise. He had to create a peace ethic for the empire to consolidate and thrive, now that it had been brought together by an ethic of war. Of the traditions in India during that time, Buddhism offered the strongest institutional base, with its network of the monastic-centered religious community, its popular literature, and its well-developed educational program aimed at instructing the laity as well as monks and nuns. Buddhism presented a middle way between hard-nosed utilitarian political thought and traditional Brahmin religious thought, so it was natural that the Buddhists would be the community of choice for Ashoka.

Ashoka's social philosophy seems to have been extracted from Buddhism and implemented and maintained by the force of his enormous personal power and prestige. Although Ashoka's efforts were countered by his immediate successors, they created a momentum that eventually produced further results in India. They marked the landscape with trees planted along roads for travelers, and *stupa* monuments to enlightenment at every crossroads. They set a social style of tolerance and admiration of nonviolence. They made the community a secure establishment that became unquestioned in its ubiquitous presence as school for gentleness, concentration, and liberation of critical reason; asylum for nonconformity; egalitarian democratic community, where decisions were made by consensual vote; and haven of mental and spiritual peace. It is no accident that Mahatma Gandhi, the modern father of the politics of nonviolence, arose in India. It is significant that he chose Ashoka's lion pillar, surmounted by the Wheel of Dharma, as the symbol to be enshrined on the flag of the newly independent nation. Ashoka's institutionalization of the Buddha's inner revolution serves as the political foundation for the psychological flexibility and social wisdom that have made it possible for India to continue to function as the largest democracy in the world, despite all its problems.

By analyzing Ashoka's edicts, we can discern five basic principles at the heart of a politics of enlightenment, now as then: (1) transcendental individualism, (2) nonviolence, (3) educational evolutionism, (4) social altruism, and (5) universal democratism.

1. Transcendental Individualism

Ashoka expressed his belief in the importance of the individual in one of his edicts.

It is difficult to achieve happiness, either in this life or the next life, except by intense love of truth, intense self-examination, intense obedience, intense fear of sin, and intense enthusiasm. Yet as a result of my instruction, regard for truth and love of truth have increased day by day and will continue to increase. My officials of all ranks—high, low, and intermediate—act in accord with the precepts of my instruction, and by their example and influence they are able to recall fickle-minded people to their duty. The officials of my border districts enforce my injunctions in the same way. For these are their rules: to govern according to the truth, to advance the people's happiness according to the truth, and to protect them according to the truth.

The Buddha rejected the idea that there is an irreducible core of personality that is independent, fixed, and indivisible. His enlightenment emerged from seeing through the illusion of a static individual entity at the core of self. He recognized himself as a fluctuating, relative process of mental and physical life, totally interconnected with all levels of the environment. But the key point is that the importance of the relative individual is not lessened. Its importance actually increases.

If persons were really metaphysical individuals, static units ultimately separate from all processes of life, they would be essentially isolated from those processes. They would have no leverage over them. They would be frozen in time and space, unable to function, without contact with anything outside their isolated selves. That individuals are responsible for their own destinies and can attain full freedom and enlightenment is the hallmark of enlightened social thought. Enlightenment institutions are designed to give individuals more power to determine their own goals and paths, to place the highest priority on their duty to the living self, over and above the numerous duties to others that constitute the social fabric of family, profession, clan, nation, religion, and so forth.

In practice, it might seem that everyone is thus unleashed to pursue his or her own absolute self-interest, which could lead to a state of anarchy. However, the assumption that there is such a thing as absolute self-interest arises only from the erroneous view of oneself as absolute. The enlightenment-oriented education system has shown itself quite capable of calming this distortion in large numbers of people in many societies. And for the really hard cases, the intellectuals and warriors, the monastic strategy of advanced education is there to channel the tendency to absolute self-interest toward pure freedom and supreme happiness. The discovery of selflessness ultimately satisfies self-interest because it finally resolves the individual's suffering and dissatisfaction. The discovery effects the cessation of suffering not through a program of self-interest but by curing the individual of false views of the self. Thus enlightenment and its institutions are antidotes for the exaggerated self-interest that makes all forms of social organization unlivable. This enlightenment cure does not attempt, as collectivisms do, to merely suppress or deflect everyone's self-interest—which leads to the authoritarian state. It acknowledges the presence of self-interest in the unenlightened, provides education to enlighten them, adapts to the variety of dispositions, proclaims its own highest aim to be the happiness of its individuals, and elicits the voluntarism of released and satisfied individuals.

"Transcendental individualism" describes the political principle acknowledging the supremacy of the individuals' happiness over the polity's collective needs for security, productivity, order, and celebration. That there is a supreme fulfillment gives individual life meaning and value. Only an individual's own understanding—attained through an educative process undergone with systematic effort, penetrated with creative intelligence, in a context of individual liberty—can lead to the enjoyment of peace. And once that is recognized, the collective must adopt the principle that none of its interests as a collective is as important as its individuals' interest in development toward freedom and happiness. Or, to put it another way, the collective society's own highest value is the fulfillment by individuals of their own highest good. The greatest society is that society which best enables its individual members to achieve their individual highest happiness. Each individual's highest duty is to his or her own liberty and happiness. Each one's highest duty to another is to assist him or her in achieving his or her own fullest liberty and highest happiness.

2. Nonviolence

In his Rock Edict IV, Ashoka proclaims nonviolence, the second principle of enlightened polity.

> For many hundred years in the past, slaughter of animals, cruelty to living creatures, discourtesy to relatives, and disrespect for priests and ascetics have been increasing. But now because of King Ashoka's practice of the truth, the sound of war-drums has become the call to truth, summoning the people to exhibitions of the chariots of the gods, elephants, fireworks, and other heavenly displays. King Ashoka's inculcation of truth has increased, beyond anything observed in many hundreds of years, abstention from killing animals and from cruelty to living beings, kindliness in human and family relations, respect for priests and ascetics, and obedience to mother and father and elders . . .

Nonviolence is the most immediate corollary of valuing the individual. Once the purpose of the society becomes the development of its individuals, the lives of those individuals become the most precious things imaginable to that society. To take their lives away or give them up for collective purposes of territory, wealth, power, or glory is a complete dislocation of redefined social purpose.

According to the Buddha's vision of evolution, while all sentient beings have souls and will eventually become enlightened, human life is a pinnacle of the evolutionary development of gentleness, tolerance, justice, intelligence,

concentration, and dedication. Human birth is a great opportunity earned through intense efforts and long sufferings
through limitless lifetimes in every conceivable other life-
form. If an individual should lose that life before having the
fullest chance to attain freedom, it is a tragedy that will follow him or her potentially for trillions more lifetimes. To kill
a human being while he or she is still ignorant is to sentence
him or her to die a trillion further deaths. In addition, as a result of the buildup of negativity caused by having killed, the
killer will suffer the loss of his or her life many times in the
future. To cut short the life of an enlightened person is to
deny great numbers of people access to the liberative teachings.

On the way to achieving enlightenment, it is impractical
to throw one's life away foolishly or in martyrdom. You die
before you can truly open your heart in transcendent understanding, and you allow your opponent to harm himself
and his future evolution by killing you.

Nonviolence sometimes translates into surgical violence.
There is a story of one of the Buddha's previous lives that
shows this kind of action. He was on a boat with 500 people
and discovered that one man intended to kill everyone. The
buddha-to-be killed the murderer to prevent him from committing another act of violence, thus saving the other people's lives. As a near buddha, he had extraordinary powers of
insight to be able to see that this action was best in the long
run.

On the way to total nonviolence, individuals must overcome the reflex of responding to violence with violence.
Not merely not killing but *preserving* lives is the first of Buddhism's "commandments." The ability to suffer violence lov-
ingly can come only from the enlightened vision of the
radical interconnectedness of other and self; from the vis-
ceral awareness of the transcendental happiness at the core
of our lives, at the heart of life, in the central subatomic energy in each of our hearts. It is an awareness that makes one
fearless of death, or, put another way, more afraid of hating
than dying, and able to die without losing touch with happiness.

Nonviolence toward humans cannot take firm hold in a
society as long as brutality and violence are practiced toward other animals. Enlightened awareness sees animals simply as lapsed humans, which every human subconsciously
knows. Animals also have evolved enormously from states
below theirs. They are relatively close to humans, and they
need encouragement and gentle treatment to accelerate their
evolution. In Pillar Edict V, Ashoka gives a long list of various species of animals under his protection, and bans hunt-
ing for sport. And in Rock Edict I, he records his own
struggle to overcome his addiction to meat-eating: "Many
hundreds of living creatures were formerly slaughtered every
day for the curries in the kitchens of His Majesty. At present,
when this edict on truth is being inscribed, only three living
creatures are killed daily, two peacocks and a deer, and the

deer is not slaughtered regularly. In the future, not even these three animals shall be slaughtered . . ."

This honest admission of human frailty gives us insight into the man. There is little doubt that during the Buddha's era, the agricultural economy of India was systematically discouraging the wastefulness of breeding cattle for meat instead of using the grain directly for human consumption. The meat-eating culture of the Indo-Aryan nomads had long been transformed by the realities of living in the subcontinent. Buddhism never made vegetarianism a rigid principle, as did Jainism, but Buddhism's principle of nonviolence promoted it by discouraging the slaughter of animals for food. Ashoka's edicts on this subject are historic—they mark the first use of official authority to promote vegetarianism. Although it still is not total, widespread vegetarianism is more prominent in India today than in any other country in the world.

Embracing the preeminence of the individual is key to being able to uphold nonviolence in threatening situations. Ashoka was unable to practice unilateral nonviolence and disarmament. He maintained his military, threatened border tribes with retaliation if they attacked him, and punished transgressors under his rule with great severity. A world where mass violence is held in stasis by the principle of mutually assured destruction, under which we have been living in the twentieth century, is the antithesis of a world of true peace—though it might be the threshold of mutual disarmament. Societies that have become truly civilized in the sense of behaving nonviolently, such as late-first-millennium C.E. India, the Jewish nation in exile, modern Tibet, and modern Mongolia, have been conquered or destroyed by violent neighbors, and millions of individual lives have been lost. Unilateral disarmament causes you to become totally vulnerable to your former and potential enemies. Only the transcendental understanding of reality can sustain this attitude in a nation or an individual.

3. *Educational Evolutionism*

A society geared to uncovering truth and spreading enlightened attitudes will necessarily focus intently on education, make it one of the chief preoccupations of policy. Ashoka supported the religious orders as teaching institutions and also made education a state matter.

> My officers charged with the spread of truth are occupied with various kinds of services beneficial to ascetics and householders, and they are empowered to concern themselves with all teachings. I have ordered some of them to look after the affairs of the [Buddhist] community, some to take care of the Brahmin and Ajivika ascetics, some to work among the Jains, and some among the various other faiths. Different officials are thus assigned specifically to the affairs of different religious groups, but my officers for spreading truth are occupied with all of them.

Education is the major tool of truth-conquest, as well as the most important survival technique known to man. It promotes enlightenment as the flowering of the individual's own awareness, sensibility, and powers, and thereby develops a strong society. Within the context of the politics of enlightenment, it is understood that the purpose of human life is education, not that education prepares a person for some other life-purpose. Education is a requirement for accelerating the process of evolution that brings the individual to human birth and for ensuring that he or she achieves the quantum jump of awareness from the constriction of automatic self-centeredness into the freedom of selfless relativity. Institutions are then created to deliver educational assistance to the maximum number of people with their different capacities in all their various situations. Education does not take place only in a classroom but works through language, literature, and the arts, through the popular circulation of songs and stories, and, in modern times, through the mass media. Religious institutions also are concerned with education, though all too often they lapse into indoctrination, shifting focus from bringing out people's higher qualities to fitting them into rigid molds of behavior and belief.

The people can be induced to advance in Dharma by only two means, by moral prescriptions and by meditation. Of the two, moral prescriptions are of little consequence, but meditation is of great importance. The moral prescriptions I have promulgated include rules making certain animals inviolable, and many others. But even in the case of abstention from injuring and from killing living creatures, it is by meditation practice that people have progressed in the Dharma most.

Ashoka always proclaimed the gift of teaching—education—the supreme gift. It is good to give people food and wealth, but they will consume it and eventually need more. It is good to give people security—they will be safe for a while—but eventually they will need more protection. The greatest wealth is for them to obtain the ability to acquire their own wealth. The greatest security is for them to gain the ability to protect themselves. The greatest happiness is for each of them to learn how to see clearly. Giving the education that brings out people's own understanding of themselves and their world is the gift of truth, Dharma, and that is true education.

4. Social Altruism

Social altruism describes the personal and political principle that others are as important or more important than oneself and that the collective good consists of each individual's happiness. Truly altruistic monarchs must come to think of their subjects as their primary concern and put their good first. They must come to think of their job as channeling the energies of the whole society toward the welfare of each individual, leaving out no one. These attitudes may be especially difficult for monarchs, who may be led to think of themselves as the most important persons in the kingdom, and of marginal groups as dispensable.

Prior to Ashoka, the operative theory of kingship in India was a form of rule by divine right. The king had absolute right of punishment; he was the absolute commander of the armies; he could order whole towns or provinces put to the sword if the people displeased him. Ashoka turned the role of the king into that of a father. Everyone deserved equal attention, concern, and compassion. Punishment for wrongdoing was tempered by compassion. Individual lives were supreme in value because they could develop toward freedom and enlightenment. And as we have seen, what's good for the individual can be best for everyone.

Ashoka traveled around giving gifts. He commissioned his queens and ministers to do likewise. He planted trees along the roads, built rest-houses and hospices for the poor and sick, patronized medicine, and imported doctors and herbs from as far away as Greece. He provided for convicts and their families, sent out special ministers to investigate cases of judicial harshness or corruption, and repeatedly freed prisoners on special occasions. Accounts indicate that he had inherited a harsh system of government from his militaristic predecessors and was not very successful in implementing a welfare system. He was also quite autocratic by habitual disposition. Thus it is all the more remarkable that he would adopt the principle of making the collective society responsible for each individual's welfare, providing each person the base from which to work toward his or her own fulfillment.

5. *Universal Democratism*

Universal democratism is the fifth operative principle in Ashoka's effort and is reflected in his edicts. It follows from the previous four as the institutional government style that can best implement them. Since each individual's good is the collective's primary good, since the evolution of those individuals is paramount and the collective is responsible for them, the actual delivery of those individual goods is possible only for a decentralized, adaptable executive that both knows the condition of each individual and can provide the specific support required. The monarchic form of executive Ashoka embodied was basically overwhelmed by this responsibility, though he heroically tried to explode himself into multiple embodiments through representatives. In theory, Ashoka would have been more successful if he had worked within a true democracy. In trying to impose a revolution from above on a vast empire, Ashoka seems to have been stressfully busy. His Rock Edicts VI and VIII give us some sense of his own lifestyle.

In the past, state business was not transacted or reports made at all hours of the day. I have therefore made arrangements that officials may have access to me and may report

on the affairs of my people at all times and in all places—
when I am eating, when I am in the harem or my inner
apartments, when I am attending to the cattle, or when I am
walking or engaged in religious exercises. I now attend to
the affairs of the people in all places. And when a donation
or a proclamation that I have ordered verbally or an urgent
matter which I have delegated to my high officials causes a
debate or dispute in the Council, this must be reported to
me immediately, at all hours and in all places. These are my
orders. I am never completely satisfied with my work or
my vigilance in carrying out public affairs. I consider the
promotion of the people's welfare my highest duty, and its
exercise is grounded in work and constant application. No
task is more important to me than promoting the well-being
of the people. Such work as I accomplish contributes to dis-
charging the debt I owe to all living creatures to make them
happy in this world and to help them attain heaven in the
next . . . King Ashoka does not consider glory or renown of
great value except insofar as the people, at present and in
the future, hear of his practice of the truth and [themselves]
live in accordance with that Dharma . . . For this purpose he
desires glory and fame . . .

While he exercised strong authority, Ashoka gave considerable autonomy to his provincial governors, a dangerous
thing to do in those days, as they tended to overthrow the
central regimes whenever they could. He relied on the wel-

fare and educational activities of his Dharma ministers to grant the populace enough of a stake in his regime to maintain it. He has been greatly criticized for the looseness of his administration, which may have kept his empire from lasting more than a couple of generations after him. Ashoka had hoped that his children and grandchildren would heed his edicts. His wish seems tragic in the short run, in that his own son reversed his gentle policies just to distinguish himself from his father, beginning a brutal persecution of the community, plunging the empire into confusion and violence, and bringing the dynasty to a premature end. But Ashoka's loosely held governmental reins may reflect a realistic assessment on his part of the prohibitive cost of keeping such a wealthy, diverse, and populous society under tight control. His success should not be measured primarily in terms of the longevity of the state he took over and transformed, but rather in terms of the vastness of his aims; the degree to which he put his principles into effect; his civilizing impact on the many nations of the empire; and his influence on the spread of this impact throughout Asia.

Ashoka's energetic and sweeping efforts to reform and redirect society provide a powerful lesson for us today, when we seem predisposed to consider the enlightenment movement apolitical and asocial. We consider such a movement powerless to affect the institutions of social management and political control. We do not expect such movements to develop any principles of social responsibility or institutional effectiveness. We expect power to find a natural balance with other powers, then we sit back and hope this balance will not be too destructive to the powerless.

Thomas Jefferson, Benjamin Franklin, and their colleagues taught the emerging U.S. democracy an ideal of enlightened government—that it should be of the people, by the people, and for the people; that the very purpose of government is to ensure each individual's life, liberty, and pursuit of happiness.

This great experiment now has been running for more than two centuries, largely as a result of the secularization of the Protestant ethic, itself founded on the repudiation of monasticism and the separation of the profane social realm from the sacred spiritual reality. The European Enlightenment, which culminated in the hot revolution that destroyed the old aristocratic lifestyle in the seventeenth and eighteenth centuries, was born out of the transition between the slow, cool revolution anchored in European Christian monasticism and the emerging Protestant ethic, industrial revolution, and secularized mass societies. This transition parallels the much earlier development in ancient India during the reign of Ashoka, when the Buddhist monastic cool revolution led to a top-down revolution instigated by the emperor. The important differences were that the Western, Protestant liberation based its move to change society on the destruction of monasticism, removing the ameliorating force of cool revolution, making hot revolution the only alternative. In the Indian case, the cool-revolution institutions were pushed into the forefront of the social order, where they were "heated up" by the government's forcing their wholesale expansion. The injection of heat into both processes caused abreaction in the process of change. In India, the successors of Ashoka undid his top-down revolution, persecuted the monastic institution, and reverted to violent lifestyles. In the European case, the post-Enlightenment revolutions were extremely violent and led to dictatorships in France and eventually in Germany; to violent conquest and despoliation of most of the non-European world; and finally to the world wars of the twentieth century, when primal, atavistic habits were armed with devastating modern technology.

In India, despite the violence that preceded and succeeded Ashoka, a glorious civilization emerged from his time—a civilization based on the transcendent value of the individual, nonviolence, education, altruistic socialism, and universal democratism—that influenced much of Asia to accept and put into practice these elements of a politics of enlightenment as best they could over the next millennium. The power of these principles is as great now as it was then.

Chapter 5

THE SOUL OF ENLIGHTENMENT

*A*t the end of his reign, it is said, Ashoka became obsessed with his resolve to give the whole empire to the monastic community. He was locked up by his ministers, who feared the wrath of his heirs should the aging emperor succeed. Ashoka wrote out the deed of the gift of the entire empire on a dried mango skin, using his own blood as ink, and threw this document out the window to a passing monk. The monk took it to his abbot, and the patriarchs of the community ritually accepted the kingdom from the emperor, in order to please him and let him have the merit of the gift. Then they summoned the ministers from court, explained what had happened, and sold back the whole of India to the dynasty for a handsome but relatively modest endowment.

This myth describes the effect of King Ashoka's life's work. His support of the enlightenment movement seemed too extensive to some people, and there was eventually a surface persecution of Buddhism. But while a monk can be killed, a university closed, a monument destroyed, changes in sensibility, language, and lifestyle cannot be reversed so easily. Within a few centuries of the Buddha's lifetime, the cool revolution had succeeded in its first phase of transforming society.

We have the testimony of Indian plays and novels and of contemporaneous Chinese pilgrims that great changes occurred in India in the centuries following Ashoka. Militarism was drastically diminished, women were more respected and free, wealth was relatively abundant, merchants were powerful, capital punishment was almost unheard of, Buddhist teachers were generally honored, and Buddhist teachings were widespread.

Once a cool revolution succeeds in a country, the enlightenment movement expands from its countercultural position and becomes mainstream; it becomes an establishment. On top of its disciplines of individual development and liberation, it must provide a broad social ethic and sense of purpose for the life of the whole society. The enlightenment movement had presented itself as an individual vehicle, conveying people to personal liberation one by one, aiming at the ideal of the perfected individual. Once the movement began to present itself as a universal vehicle of liberation, capable of conveying everyone to freedom and happiness, its ideal became the messiah or bodhisattva, the man or woman

who works to liberate him- or herself in order to save all beings. With that shift, the cool revolution turned into a
process of cool evolution toward a world filled with buddhas.

Freedom from the oppression of mundane obligations
through monastic renunciation allows individuals to pursue
their own education and development to the full extent of
their inclinations and abilities. But once these abilities have
been developed, what is the freedom for? How should educated individuals invest that liberty? What responsibilities
should they assume? The modern human rights tradition
doesn't address the issue of individual responsibility. It focuses instead on how to restrain governments in their oppressive uses of power. The one sure way to secure individual
rights in the long run is through the development of an ethic
that internally motivates the individuals in societies where
flagrant violations occur to take responsibility for respecting
one another's rights. That internal ethic is what drives a politics of enlightenment.

In the first century before and after the time of Christ, the
enlightenment movement in India began to manifest strongly
the new dimension of universal liberation. A whole new
class of teachings were discovered and developed, in which
the Buddha went far beyond his teaching of self-restraint and
individual liberation from the ordinary social world and
its corresponding personality structure. These teachings
preserved what the Buddha was thought to have taught
in private to the assemblies of the gods, extraterrestrial

bodhisattvas, and his leading monastic and lay disciples. The earlier scriptures described the audience for the Buddha's teachings mainly in human terms. In the universal vehicle, the field becomes vast—the Buddha reveals his profound metaphysic of total freedom based on fully encountering ultimate reality, which he discovered to be seething with the inconceivable energy of love. He opened the eyes of all to see the infinite enlightened buddhas, the inexhaustible love and divine powers of angelic bodhisattvas, beings who emanate themselves in countless guises around the universe in order to benefit and instruct all beings. He introduced the profound psychological insight concerning the bodhisattva's will to enlightenment in order to save all beings, elucidating the magically positive effect it has on life when a person's whole essential energy turns toward benefiting all. The sense of connectedness achieved in enlightenment expands limitlessly, leading logically to the conception of the spirit of universal responsibility—each individual's sense that he or she can act to transform the entire universe to free all beings from pain.

The new universal vehicle presents the Buddha as focused on the transformation of the entire universe, on the perfect development of a buddhaverse, an enlightened realm like the one he revealed to his disciple by pointing his toe and showing that the world contains the perfect conditions for achieving such a state. Individuals are to seek not only their personal liberation from suffering but also the liberation and perfection of their entire environment. The individual's in-exorable interconnection with all other beings is brought to the fore of awareness at the very moment one decides to embark on the quest for enlightenment. The ambition for the freedom and bliss of enlightenment thus aims at the simultaneous enlightenment of self and others. The individual vows to become enlightened with all those beings, no matter how long it may take—to become a buddha in a buddhaverse. A person who undertakes that heroic enterprise is called a bodhisattva hero or heroine of enlightenment, whose magnificent ambition to help the world transform itself is praised as a new spirit, a new soul, a luminous center of being opening on an infinite horizon of positive potential. As the Buddha left behind a method for understanding the lack of fixed identity, so he left a method for transforming the individual into a bodhisattva and then into a buddha, and for transforming the world into a buddhaverse. As always, the change begins with the individual and the individual's ability to deal with attachment and identity.

The greatest obstacle to manifesting a politics of enlightenment is in helping individuals develop an altruism that goes beyond good works to the desire to take responsibility for ending the suffering of other beings. As long as our culture is driven by individuals grasping after external stimuli to feed selves we continue to see as solid, we never will be able to become an enlightened society. We know already that we will continue to suffer as long as we are trapped by negative thoughts and feelings, and as long as we see our individual suffering as the only suffering, we lose the greatest opportunity for happiness we can have in our lives. Of all the negativities that bring us suffering, selfish desire is one of the more difficult for us to overcome. Cultivating joyous altruism can act as an antidote to this kind of suffering.

How badly are we addicted to our mundane comforts? Quite badly. First, there are the conventionally addictive things. If you have been nicotine-addicted or alcohol-addicted, you know well the meaning of addiction. We can be addicted also to prescription drugs, sex, tranquilizers, fashion, and experiences.

The automobile addiction is particularly draining. The cost to repurchase our cars part by part, which we have to do to keep them running, is often several times the original purchase price. The cost of gas, oil, and insurance, the tax cost of the road systems, the cost of the medical effort to heal those maimed in accidents—the total cost of the automobile addiction reaches into the trillions of dollars.

Clothing, electronics, entertainment—our eyes, ears, and minds are endlessly assaulted by the demand that we acquire ever-new machines to enter greater networks and communities of consumption.

The point is that in our endless pursuit of external stimuli, we waste and consume without finding satisfaction.

When did a new car ever make us permanently happy? A new lover? A new piece of clothing? The pleasure is as fleeting as the original desire to consume, pushing us to look outward all the more. The key to ending this cycle is to discover the source of discontent and realize that it will never be fulfilled. Once we stop working for the boss that's never satisfied, we may then freely choose to enjoy something without suffering at its loss, without the urgent desire for more—in other words, without addiction. Then we can experience true enjoyment. This is the inner version of the cool revolution.

We can gradually develop a coolness about our hotly desired objects, love relationships, and possessions not by giving them up but by cultivating within a lasting peace and contentment. It is not that we must withdraw suddenly from such desires. Instead, we can change the *quality* of those desires, let *them* serve *us* as our creative inspirations, rather than us serve them as addictive compulsions. In fact, we have a better chance of getting what we want when we are calmer about our wanting.

Contentment is a precious jewel, far more valuable than possession of priceless properties. It is, after all, what we are really searching for when we pursue our desires. It is a state we are already familiar with. Recall a time when you were feeling happy and mellow and then you got stuck in a traffic jam or the kitchen got flooded. Externally, the situation was bad. But internally you still felt good. Or consider an opposite situation: at a party, with people you love, in a beautiful place, when you couldn't cheer up because an earlier fight with a loved one still held you in its grip.

What do such experiences prove? That outer conditions do not make us happy or sad. They do affect us, but our inner predispositions, our subjective states themselves, are the primary determinants of the quality of our experiences. Others do not force us to have good or bad feelings, though they can please or frustrate us. We can choose to be unmoved by pleasing acts of theirs, and we can rise above any frustration. If we can understand and master the forces that create our moods, we can ensure that we are in good moods no matter what.

The study and practice—the meditation—of contentment is a gradual yoking, a change of direction that brings small but appreciable results and that constantly increases our state of well-being. When we meditate, we stop our constant focus on habitual thoughts of dissatisfaction and frustration. Sitting quietly and listening carefully to yourself, you can observe the main voice in which your thoughts recite themselves. Just by listening you gain a little free space for yourself and you no longer need to react according to the dictates of the inner voice. When you cultivate awareness of the nature of the self (see chapter 2), you will see that you are other than that dictating voice. You can gain the distance to be able to choose whether or how to react.

Once we penetrate the stream of thoughts, we experience

a silence, out of which emerges a spring of joy. This space becomes accessible when you let go of your thoughts without
commenting on them, let the inner voice go silent instead of
marching to its orders. In moments like this, a well of good
feeling rises up for no particular reason. Thoughts coming
from that silent freedom have a feel of originality, of play-
fulness. They do not drag us along by their own momentum.

This kind of reflection soon leads us to awareness of the
transitoriness of all our feelings, moods, and thoughts. The
more we see their fluctuations, the looser is their grip on us.
Even stubborn obsessions dissipate in a moment's distraction. An idea about the world that holds us in its grip one
minute is gone during a conversation in the next. People to
whom we pledge undying love or friendship can easily turn
into enemies or drop out of our lives. The mind produces
solid images and feelings that evaporate the minute the heat
of awareness is turned to them.

Faced with the fluidity of nature, we can bemoan the feeling of having the rug pulled out from under us, or we can
choose to contemplate the fleetingness of satisfaction and
pleasure, of sorrow and anger. Contemplating the falling of
the cherry blossoms in spring, the autumn wind stripping the
trees of their orange leaves, thinking of loved ones who have
grown old and perhaps the gray hairs on our own heads helps
us become more at ease with impermanence. Thinking about
our own deaths can release us from the fear of losing our

own lives—which could be gone at any moment. You can imagine your eyes unable to see, your ears unable to hear, a roar in your inner ear as a pain sears your heart and you are gone from your body. After a while, you will be only an occasional memory for the people you knew.

When you realize that you can't predict how long you will live, your relation to things becomes more relaxed, more appreciative, and yet more detached. "Death is the mother of beauty; hence from her,/Alone, shall come fulfilment to our dreams/And our desires," said the poet Wallace Stevens. By accepting impermanence, we let go of our tight grasp on what and whom we love, and knowing it or they will be gone, we see more clearly what it is we love about them.

As we look more deeply into the fluctuating natures of mind and reality, we lose the sense of their solidity, which brings us more ease. We look at a table and see that it has not only no fixed "self" as a table but, on a quantum level, no fixed solidity at all. The subatomic particles that make up matter whirl through space like tiny galaxies—vast distances between each particle, perceivable as solid only because of our gross sense of sight and touch. The illusion of substantiality dissolves before our very eyes. That car, or that person we wanted so much, is now a vibrating mass of space. It disappears with critical thinking; it releases us from our need.

Out of this spaciousness, out of this contentedness, comes also a painful awareness of the hollowness of what we once thought so solid—our desires, our thoughts, our beliefs, our very lives. There is so much to be examined, and so much of it hinges on who we think we are and what we think we need to hang on to.

We feel ourselves as individuals, irreducible someones, by identifying ourselves by race, sex, age, and religion; by ideology, nation, culture, profession, and health; by knowledge, skills, achievements, and experiences. These labels only ensure that we remain strangers to many aspects of our real selves and deeply alienated from one another. When we naively believe we are unique, independent, self-subsisting entities, essentially apart from all other persons and things, all relationship becomes problematic. Taking for granted our indubitable sense of self, we cannot count on anyone else; each person thinks he or she is the only indubitable one. No one ever can truly appreciate us and our indubitability. This is what alienation means, that everything else seems "other," that each one sees a world in which he or she is the best, the only good one. Each self-identification as the best leads to a prejudice that all the others are worse.

All of us have these prides and prejudices—except for those who have dismantled them through careful investigation and sustained meditation. These forms of pride and prejudice reinforce our senses of alienation, fear, and aloneness. They are crippling to our societies, for they prevent cooperative action and provide fault lines through which violence and waste erupt.

Pride keeps us from seeing that we all have been in the same boat in various forms and transformations during time without end. Each person can go on interminably laboring under the delusion of being separately one against all, each loving only his or her self and feeling the focus of the hate of every other. Or we can realize our relatedness to all, that we are made up of one another's molecules, we breathe them in, we absorb them in our food, we are recycled and physically affected by everything around us. My self, empty of separate self, is no different from someone else's emptiness of self. In a world where each person is all for all, each may find no separate self to love, but each has everyone else on his or her side, and each becomes the focus of infinite love. Thus, in the universe of boundless lives in space and time, every being finds ultimate release from the prison of self-concern in the energy of universal responsibility for others.

This is the spirit of enlightenment, and in a very real sense it is a new soul. The spirit of enlightenment is a kind of spiritual "gene" of universal compassion marking the quality and tendency of one's further evolution, in this life, in life after life. One gains it by conceiving the will to freedom in order to benefit all beings, and ever after the quality of one's experience and even one's biological continuum are marked by it.

This enlightening soul or spirit of enlightenment encompasses a special type of love for all that is living. It has two aspects: aspiring and actualizing. Its aspirational form is generated from insight and resolve—insight that there is such a thing as evolutionary perfection in enlightenment, that there are beings who have actually attained perfect wisdom and universal love toward all and who are really competent to help all beings; and resolve that you could and should yourself become such a person in order to help all fellow beings. Once this aspirational enlightenment-soul has become stable and intense, you formally dedicate the total energy of your life and all future lives to attaining the ability to accomplish the complete welfare, liberty, and happiness of every living being.

Thus, bodhisattvas can be seen as those who logically and courageously aim to become working messiahs (we'll use "bodhisattva" here to avoid the cultural freight weighing down the word "messiah"). The grand insight of the spirit of enlightenment is that each of us is responsible for all of us, so we all can become leaders in the great effort toward a salvation in which we do not merely seek escape but strive to become fully awake and loving of one another.

Advanced bodhisattvas, who are themselves also buddhas, achieve celestial freedom and may be considered effective liberators or saviors whom enlightenment-oriented people entreat for help in escaping the interminable suffering of the egocentric life cycle. There are innumerable less-developed bodhisattvas who work for all beings according to their abilities. Some of them strive toward enlightenment in animal embodiments; some persist in human lifetimes in all civilizations on all planets in all universes; some enter divine lifetimes in the heavens to stir the gods out of their sensory pleasures and spiritual complacency. The first bodhisattva mentioned in the Indian enlightenment literature is Shakyamuni Buddha himself in his former lives. In a collection of tales, the central figure (who will someday become the Buddha) is always a noble leader—a monkey king, a deer prince, or a chief elephant—who constantly sacrifices for others' welfare. In story after story, the point is made that the truest way to be kingly is to give yourself to your companions in service.

The power of the enlightened being to affect his or her environment is immense. The enlightened mind can landscape worlds, preserve planets, save whole environments, create buddhaverses. The enlightened being is almost like a god. He or she is creative but not "the Creator," competent and powerful in the work of liberating others, but not omnipotent.

Many individual beings have been bodhisattvas and have already become buddhas. There are countless bodhisattvas present throughout the universe striving to save, free, and help living beings. Because there is impermanence, there is no eternal damnation. The Buddha showed that each of us has the potential to become what he became—not only humans but all beings can be liberated, yet each one is responsible for his or her own liberation. There is no original Creation or beginning of the world. Rather, individual and collective karmic evolution operates beginninglessly to cause and condition particular destinies. All conditions can be corrected to the point of perfection. There is no more positive tradition than this.

Conceiving the soul of enlightenment, like understanding the emptiness of self, does not happen overnight. There are systematic methods for doing so that are especially treasured for their effectiveness in helping the individual cultivate tolerance and empathy through overcoming alienation. In this yoga, we deepen the experience of freedom by dissolving the apparent solidity of our perceptions. In the process of opening our minds, we loosen our grips on our thought and behavior patterns. Once our energies become freer from habitual perceptions and involuntary reactions, the creative power of the imagination is released.

The Indian master Asanga (fourth century) discovered seven meditational steps for cultivating this mind. They are: (1) recognition of all beings as having been one's mother; (2) remembering all their kindnesses; (3) grateful resolve to repay their kindnesses; (4) great love that wills their happiness; (5) great compassion that wills their freedom from suffering; (6) universal responsibility that resolves to save them all; and (7) the resulting soul of enlightenment, which fuses together the first six in the determination to join the buddhas in working for the good of all beings.

We begin this meditation with the understanding of the premise that oneself and all other beings have had beginningless former lives. The idea gives one a sense of the boundlessness of the horizon of life, in the past in time, in the present in space, and in the future in both time and space. Though the premise requires you to commit to some sort of belief in continuity, you need not hold an abstract, dogmatic belief in reincarnation. You can feel a sense of connection as viscerally as you feel the solidity of the earth. One cannot embrace all beings and develop boundless love if one indulges in a conviction that one is originally, essentially, or ultimately disconnected from it all, by not having existed at some time in the past, by being essentially isolated, or by becoming obliterated at death. All three of these ideas subtly intertwine to give you the same sense of alienation in the immediate present. People strongly committed to scientific materialism could perhaps find a route to something like this sense of interconnectedness by meditating on the genetic interconnection of all living species, the interchangeability of atoms among all forms, the emergence of all energies from the lump of matter that exploded in the Big Bang, and so forth. People with great faith in God can, of course, find interconnectedness with all life through its common nature of being created by God.

Your first step in the actual meditation is to cultivate impartiality. You meditate on a friend, an enemy, and a neutral stranger, seeing the temporariness of your present relations with them. Friends can become enemies; someone we hardly pay attention to now can become the beloved. Additionally, all are essentially equal in their desire for happiness and in their limitless potential as living beings. Once you establish impartiality, you can begin to contemplate your mother in this life. You recognize your connection with her, that you were conceived in, carried in, and born from her womb. While feeling these deep emotions of biological connection, you reflect that every other being has borne you in his or her womb, since we all have existed in innumerable former lives. You start with human females like your own mother, move on to females of other species, to human and animal males (first recognizing that they have had many former lives as females), and you continue until you can relate imaginatively to all species of living beings as a child to its mother. Yes, even to the cockroach, the spider, every sentient being. This action culminates in a profound emotional experience of the biological unity of all living beings.

Once you establish this unity, you concentrate on re-trieving the deep memories of the tender love and care of your mother of this lifetime—whether you got along with her or not. Most likely she would have jumped in front of you to save you from an oncoming car, or done anything else to save your life. In fact, she did save your life by feeding you and caring for you as a helpless infant. You reflect on all her kindnesses and then imagine all living beings having shown you the same tender love.

In the third step, your concentration moves from the sense of unity and deep emotional appreciation into the welling up of the strong wish to do something for all these "mother" beings out of gratitude, to repay their infinite kindnesses.

The fourth step, intensifying this love, comes in the form of wishing for the happiness of all beings, contemplating all of them one by one—beginning with those you are closest to—and thinking of what it takes to make them happy, visualizing their pleasure as they receive what they most need. You begin to realize that there are few things that can produce any lasting happiness and that these dear beings will be really happy only when they have achieved their own freedom and enlightenment.

The fifth step, compassion, ensues from the moment you open yourself to the actual sufferings your innumerable mothers are constantly undergoing. You see them sick and injured, disappointed and bereaved, old and feeble and despondent. You see them terrified and desperate, facing death and torment. If you have opened to the worldview of endless lifetimes, you see them suffering the pains of repeated deaths and rebirths in various forms of life; burning or freezing in hells; thirsting and starving; being crushed and trapped as insects, worms, or rodents. When you open yourself to the immense tragedy of ordinary life cycles, you can feel a tearing grief, a rawness of agony, a shudder at the unbearable suffering of this infinite mass of living beings to whom you now know you are intimately connected.

Then you pass into a kind of hypersensitivity, a burning

impulse to do something, anything, to lessen the great mass of suffering that is the ordinary life cycle as beings habitually experience it. We each take upon ourselves the overwhelming burden of responsibility for doing something about the condition of all our mothers. The pressure squeezes out all trivial concerns, and we become filled with the high resolve of universal responsibility.

There is only one kind of being capable of helping others to end their suffering, and that is a fully enlightened buddha. A buddha has the experience, the tools, the wisdom, and the boundless compassion for accomplishing this task. Nothing else has any importance; nothing must deter you; you must become the sole caretaker of all helpless living beings. At the same time you feel this determination, however, it is crucial that you keenly feel your inability to carry it out at this time. You realize you need complete freedom from afflictions yourself, as well as virtual omniscience about the conditions of others so that you know exactly how to help. You need to know the techniques to lead a sufferer to happiness. And you need a perfect impartiality toward all others, coupled with a complete selflessness. In short, you must become a perfect buddha.

The emotional crescendo builds to the seventh step, wherein insight and faith combine. The insight is that already there have been infinite numbers of beings who have come this way, who have realized the organic relatedness of all life and have taken up the high resolve, who have practiced all the stages of the path and even have attained buddhahood. They have realized the ability to do that which you and I are resolved to do. They already have seen the liberation and bliss of all beings in the timeless context of their inconceivable knowledge. With the sense of grace from their presence, you perceive the situation as less overwhelming, less desperate, and you can calm the panic exploding within you in the face of universal responsibility. Your will is still focused toward the attainment of buddhahood, on the aim to join the ranks of those competent to alleviate the sufferings of beings. But your intensity of will is now balanced with your sense of the grace and the blessings of the buddhas, whose presence and goodwill surround you in luminous embrace.

Modern psychology considers this kind of messianic spirit troublesome because it has no way of understanding the diffused ego. But when you hold the enlightenment view of reality, operating from such a spirit is without a doubt the soundest, most energetic way to be. Which view is the accurate one? The materialist critique of spiritual awakening as an illusion? Or the enlightenment critique of habitual materialism as illusory? Consider, for the moment, this version of Pascal's wager. If conscious life is a random and meaningless exercise, if our person has come from an inexplicable origin for no purpose and is scheduled for eventual oblivion, no one will be around to regret having made the effort to construct a meaning and purpose for wisdom, love, and happiness. No one will regret the wasted time. But if the alienated consciousness rooted in materialism is the illusion, if life is a great field of awareness with infinite continuity which can be bottomlessly miserable or boundlessly happy, and if one does not use the human lifetime to the full, changing negative emotions to positive ones, then oneself and all interconnected conscious life will deeply regret this tragic waste. This wager can be sufficiently compelling to set us to work on the turn to the positive through the will to enlightenment, until such time as we actually experience the interconnectedness of life, an experience that is not all that difficult to attain.

Our current psychology sees the bodhisattva spirit as a form of mental illness, a dangerous delusion that can lead a person to self-destruction through feeling helpless in the face of all others' suffering. If we have only one life to live, we can undertake only a limited number of activities and have very little responsibility beyond our skins or even to ourselves. In that case, the judgment is sound. The sentient beings that we can see even on this planet are too numerous for us to help. So how could we ever benefit an infinite number of beings?

For an individual who is encouraged to come to an existential resignation in the face of a senseless, pointless existence, there is no purpose for doing anything but pursuing immediate gratification. Without karma, there are no consequences, and without a future, no ability to progress. There is no reason at all to conceive a grand scheme to save the whole living universe. Such a scheme might temporarily energize the personality, but it would seem utterly unrealistic. Such a resolution would put us under unbearable stress, spoil our self-respect, our relations with others, and lead to futile megalomania. This view belongs to modern psychology.

From the enlightenment view of space/time reality as infinite, of life as boundless, and of our connections to it and to all beings within it as beyond measure, the spirit of enlightenment and the universal vehicle are quite logical. Each of us is rooted in all things, and all things are rooted in each of us.

The evolutionary dedication of the man or woman bodhisattva, the enlightening hero or heroine, is given in the form of a vow. It expresses the resolve you feel at the moment when you first conceive the spirit or soul of enlightenment. It has been recited as a prayer by millions of enlightenment-oriented people in Asia over the centuries, in the form given it by the great eighth-century Buddhist poet Shantideva.

By the virtue amassed by all that I have done,
May the pain of every being be completely healed.
May I be doctor and medicine, and may I be nurse
For all sick beings in the world, 'til all are well.
May food and drink rain down to stop all thirst and hunger,
And during times of famine, may I turn myself into food and
    drink.

May I be an endless treasure for the poor and destitute;
May I turn into all things they could ever need,
And may these then be placed close beside them.
With no sense of loss, may I give up possessions, even my body,
And all past, present, and future virtues, to help all beings. . . .
May I be savior of those without one, a guide for all the lost,
A bridge, a ferry, and a ship for all who cross the water.
May I be an island for those who seek one, and a lamp for those
*   desiring light.*
May I be a bed for all who wish to rest, and a slave for all who
*   want a slave.*
May I be a wishing jewel, a magic vase, powerful mantras, and
*   great medicine,*
May I become a wish-fulfilling tree, and a cow of plenty for the
*   world. . . .*
'Til they pass from pain, may I also be the source of life
For all realms of beings to the end of space.
Just as all former Lords of Bliss conceived this enlightened spirit
And progressively performed the bodhisattva deeds,
So for the sake of all beings, I, too, conceive this enlightened
*   spirit,*
And so will I, too, progressively perform these deeds.

This is the messianic drive of the bodhisattva, the spirit of
love and compassion called the enlightening soul. It is not
merely the wish that all be well with all beings—it is the determination that you yourself will assume responsibility for

others. Acting on the insight that yourself and others actually are one single body of life and that your sense of having
a self apart is a tragic illusion, you joyfully wish to give yourself away totally, on every level, to enrich the lives of all. You
systematically resolve to attain buddhahood, which is the ultimate form of evolution, the state from which you really can
accomplish the benefit of living beings.

The magnificent conception of this soul of enlightenment
is a central moment in the evolutionary career of a sentient
being. It is the moment in which a new spirit of love and
compassion pervades the being's whole life and destiny, and
further evolution becomes a purposive, creative progress.
Shantideva stated that as soon as beings conceive this soul of
enlightenment, they become "children of the Lord of Bliss,"
each a buddhachild. From this moment, they become bodhisattvas, worthy of honor, who can rejoice in the newfound
fruitfulness of their existence.

It is impossible to overemphasize the enhancement of life
brought about by the conception of this soul of enlightenment. It is a conscious act of making one's own life
purposeful and, by experiencing unconditional love and
compassion, of easing the suffering of others everywhere.
From the moment one attains this grand conception, one
has an inexhaustible well of hope and optimism. One must
become open to the prospect of boundless future existences.
Then the horizon is vast and open-ended enough that the
bodhisattva does not feel excessive pressure and the mes-

sianic orientation indeed becomes reasonable, natural, and even immediately rewarding. This is the yoga of the greatest contentment, wherein we turn away from the self to find the doorway to happiness and the most powerful form of inner revolution.

Chapter 6

THE POWER OF
COOL HEROISM

One of the main leaders of the universal enlightenment movement in India was a great monk-teacher called Nagarjuna, who lived sometime between the first century B.C.E. and the second century C.E. By this time, India had developed enormously, with large numbers of enlightened individuals working to transform the whole society gradually. Nagarjuna became a monk as a young child, and later became a famous monastic teacher, a medical doctor, and an alchemist. Legend also casts Nagarjuna in a unique role as rediscoverer of the teachings of the universal vehicle itself, said to have been lost to humanity since the Buddha's time.

Myth has it that one day, Nagarjuna recognized two dragons posing as humans at the back of his lecture hall. After the class, he called them over and asked why they had come to see him. They invited him down to their realm at the bottom of the Indian Ocean to visit the dragon king's palace. There the dragon king's daughter showed him a treasure room, where the scriptures recording the Buddha's universal-liberation teachings were stored in rich profusion. After fifty years of earth time studying these teachings, Nagarjuna brought them out of the sea's depths and returned with them to India.

Nagarjuna used his position as a famed and respected teacher of monastic Buddhism to spread these teachings widely. He eventually became the mentor of a great king of a dynasty in southern India, King Udayi Shatavahana, who ruled the area of the Deccan highland running from contemporary Bombay to Andhra Pradesh (ca. 150–200 C.E.). Though the archaeological, artistic, and literary evidence of the king's rule is only fragmentary, the advice that Nagarjuna gave to King Udayi has come down to us in Nagarjuna's famous text the *Jewel Garland of Royal Counsel,* which was probably written around mid–second century C.E.*

---

*When cool revolution has attained a certain level of success, it changes into cool evolution. The countercultural monastic movement no longer needs to lie low and is able to give the ruling powers advice, spiritual and social. Enlightened sages can begin to advise their royal disciples on how to conduct the daily affairs of society, such as what should be their policies and practices. Likewise, after a long period of such evolution, the entire movement can reach a cool fruition, when the countercultural enlightenment movement becomes mainstream and openly takes responsibility for the whole society, which eventually happened in Tibet. It is squarely in the center of all enlightened traditions to bring basic principles to bear on actual contemporary problems in order to

Nagarjuna instructed the king first in what he needed to know for his own liberation and development, in line with Ashoka's first principle of enlightened politics, the transcendent value of the individual. Nagarjuna then advised King Udayi on the basic principle of enlightened social action, the universal altruism of great love and great empathy: "O King! Just as you love to consider what to do to help yourself, so should you love to consider what to do to help others!" He taught his friend the king how to care for every being in his kingdom: by building schools everywhere and endowing honest, kind, and brilliant teachers; by providing for all his subjects' needs, opening free restaurants and inns for travelers; by tempering justice with mercy, sending barbers, doctors, and teachers to the prisons to serve the inmates; by thinking of each prisoner as his own wayward child, to be corrected in order to return to free society and use his or her precious human life to attain enlightenment.†

---

develop ethical, even political, guidelines for action. This activism is implicit in the earliest teachings of the Buddha and in his actions, though his focus at that time was on individual self-transformation, the prerequisite of social transformation. The importance of universal transformation becomes fully explicit in the magnificent description of the bodhisattva career.

†Nagarjuna showed King Udayi how the simplest local action radically changes when it becomes part of a universal enterprise—the individual's sense of infinite participation is the essential ecological energy. People's minds and hearts are the most powerful and precious

Following Nagarjuna's advice, King Udayi was able to implement the principles of enlightened politics in his kingdom more completely, in fact, than Ashoka had because of this introduction of universal responsibility.

In addition, Nagarjuna said that if a ruler cannot implement a politics of enlightenment, then that ruler must abandon the throne to pursue enlightenment first. This counsel contradicts all other systems of political wisdom, which posit the ruler and the ruler's work as the most important. The "sacred duty" of the king, the "supreme responsibility" of the president—so much that supports the insufferable pompousness of rulers derives from the idea that the will and the need of the collective are supreme over the will and need of the individual. The prime self-sacrificer is said to be the ruler himself or herself—"Heavy lies the head that wears the crown." The king must put the collective ahead of himself, submerge his individual interest in the collective interest, and in so doing confirm that all individuals in the society matter less than the collective will. This is the essence of the

---

energies of nature. When they are in balance, their harmony with nature will cause everything to flourish. The *Jewel Garland* says that when nature is treated well, it will serve the people well, and even the weather is said to favor such a society, the rains coming on time and in proper measure.

Translations from *Jewel Garland* adapted from original Sanskrit and Tibetan translations; a full English translation is available in Nagarjuna, *Precious Garland* (Somerville, MA: Wisdom Publications, 1997).

totalitarian state, whether fascist, communist, or imperialist. Individual fulfillment is suppressed in the name of the liberation of all the people, but the bottom line is that not a single one gets liberated. There is no way to liberate people other than one by living one, and, according to Nagarjuna's advice, starting with the king himself.

The practical impact of this advice is that the immediate needs of the collective are just not that important. The collective interest is no more than the sum of the individual interests. No matter how much territory a society acquires, how much glory or wealth, each individual within it still will sicken, age, and die. The collective cannot help that individual beyond death. Only by our understanding the lack of fixed identity and reaching mastery of our reactions through meditation can we help our situation. It is the job of society to provide the individual with the opportunity to cultivate these abilities. More than two-thirds of the *Jewel Garland* contains personal instructions on realizing the core insight of individualism, the freedom from a rigid, unchanging self.

By combining the insight into the nature of self with universal responsibility, Nagarjuna added a new dimension not only to the evolution of Buddhism but to the unfolding of Indian society itself. Evidence of King Udayi's success at implementing the five principles of the politics of enlightenment—transcendent value of the individual, nonviolence, educational evolutionism, social altruism, and universal democratism—can be found in sources like the *Flower Garland*

Sutra, the literature of south India, the art of Ajanta and Amaravati, the accounts of Chinese pilgrims, and Tibetan histories. It was a civilization of wealthy cities, powerful monasteries, luxurious courts of great sensuous refinement, widespread scholarship, intense asceticism, prosperous farmers and peasants, relatively long-lasting peace, and political stability.

In the late third and early fourth centuries C.E., the Gupta family began a drive to reestablish an indigenous Indian dynasty in northern India, in the Gangetic and Indus heartland. At that time, India was a huge subcontinent with a population at least ten times that of all Europe. It held many nations speaking different languages, meaning that regionalized forms of governance constituted its natural state. It took an extraordinary effort to gather the whole of it together under a single administration. The Gupta synthesis of classical Indian culture unified Buddhism and Vedism and gave birth to what has come to be called Hinduism. That empire lasted until the sixth century C.E., when it finally gave way to various regional empires.

With minor exceptions, all Indian empires of the early centuries C.E. supported the expansion of the Buddhist community while simultaneously patronizing Hindu gods. They funded the monastic universities, offered elaborate monuments or additions to the famous stupas commemorating the events of the Buddha's life, and supported major public works such as painted-cave temples and monasteries.

In the fifth through the seventh centuries C.E., the Chinese monk-explorers I Tsing and Hsuan Tsang traveled throughout Central Asia, Southeast Asia, and India and recorded the world they encountered. Militarism was not much in evidence, and capital punishment was almost unheard of: Though law and order were questionable in many parts, and robbers posed great dangers for the traveler, elaborate penal codes were not seen as useful deterrents to crime. Thriving communities of monks and nuns stretched from one end of the subcontinent to the other. Books were widely available, and learned teachers were to be met with in every important town.

During this first millennium C.E., India underwent a progressive civilizing process wherein individualism was furthered to an unprecedented degree. Militarism was diminished, and the civilization as a whole approached unilateral disarmament in terms of the conditions of warfare of the time. Education in general, and especially spiritually evolutionist education, was universally available and highly desirable. The subcontinent became known all over Asia as the Holy Land of the Buddha and his community. It attracted all manner of reverent pilgrims and earnest students, and the monarchs became renowned more for their patronage of spiritual monuments and institutions of learning than for their exploits of conquest. So, what began as a militaristic empire powerful enough to beat back Alexander the Great evolved into a peaceful land of wealth and beauty.

However, at the end of the first millennium C.E., the over-all gentleness of the fully developed enlightenment-oriented Indian civilization attracted large-scale systematic invasions by various central Asian tribes, newly unified by a militant Islam. These invasions destroyed the Buddhist monastic universities, and the entire character of the civilization was set back into an ideologically intolerant, militaristic mode.

That intolerance can overwhelm tolerance both in individuals and in nations is a harsh reality, but it need not discourage us. Rather, that painful reality can encourage us to direct our efforts toward developing tolerance. The cultivation of tolerance is the foundation of cool heroism and provides the firmest basis for a politics of enlightenment.

You can cultivate tolerance by understanding your biological connection to others through the meditation on seeing all as having been your mother (see chapter 5), and also by meditatively putting yourself into someone else's psychic shoes. Cultivation of tolerance, which leads to compassionate behavior, follows a precise pattern of development: (1) contemplating the faults of hate; (2) contemplating the benefits of tolerance; (3) preventing the cause of hate; (4) meditating on tolerating voluntary suffering; (5) meditating on tolerance grounded in the awareness of reality; and (6) meditating on the tolerance of nonretaliation.

"Hate" and "anger" often are used interchangeably. I will

use "hate" for the mental and spiritual poison that wants to see others destroyed, and "anger" for the state of vigorous energy that determines to right a wrong situation. Anger combines sometimes with hate and sometimes with love. When anger is aligned with compassion, it is cool anger, forceful and vigorous but not hot and searing to the core. Force and even fierceness may be used to clear away an obstacle, but not to harm intentionally. However, when anger is aligned with hate, the person goes berserk, loses self-control, and hurts others and even himself or herself. Some modern psychologists have discovered that anger as an agent of love can be very useful for relieving internal or external oppression, and many people have used it to free themselves from oppressive situations.

On the other hand, we ought to beware the pop-psychology idea that anger is a fixed quantity of energy that must be used up—you either express it outwardly by defending yourself from oppressions, or you repress it and turn it inward, which adds self-loathing to oppression by others. Therefore, it is said to be essential for you to loose it on the world to avoid bottling it up and harming yourself. All this shows us is how drastically we have been taught to misinterpret our experience. We confuse forcefulness and aggressiveness with anger and hatred. We don't realize we can be much more forceful without anger, much more effectively aggressive without hatred. These are the first lessons of any authentic martial art. You de-identify yourself as victim, and you do not identify the other as willfully attacking. You perceive the attack against you as blind, impersonal forces that have gone out of control. You can then intervene coolly to turn those forces back on themselves.

To master anger, it is crucial that you clear up this confusion. Exploding in anger is not the sign of righteous resistance to oppression—it is the final capitulation to oppression, the surrender of free consciousness and controlled forcefulness to blind impulse.

There is nothing more evil than hate. Long years of good work can go to waste because of a single spasm of hate. You may have spent a long time cultivating a relationship, and one day you become confused and perceive that friend as an enemy to your happiness. You suddenly explode in anger, lose control, and hurt your friend verbally or physically. We hear about this every day in circumstances ranging from domestic violence to all-out war.

The great mass killings of this century—the murder of the Armenians; the slaughter in the trenches of World Wars I and II; the forced starvations in Africa; the Holocaust of the European Jews; the Japanese extermination of Manchurians and Chinese; the Tibetan, Cambodian, and Rwandan genocides; the imprisonment and executions of Native Americans and African Americans—all these horrors have had hate as their root and persistent cause. If there is a nuclear holocaust that ends all life on this planet, it will not be caused by nuclear technology or by political, religious, or economic disagreements. It will be caused by hate. The energy moving the hand that signs the order to build missiles is that of hate. And in the final moment, the force that moves the finger to press the button to launch those missiles is none other than hate. Hate now can destroy all life on earth.

In the karmic evolutionary sense, the positive imprints of virtuous actions, the seeds of future insight and freedom planted by the work of learning, reflection, and contemplation, all the positive developmental energy we accumulate in a lifetime of effort can be destroyed by hate. It is said that hate can create an instant hell, a nightmare death, and a horrific wakening.

Evolutionary effects may be a somewhat obscure concept for our usual one-life outlook, but we all can easily comprehend murder, warfare, and mass destruction. On the individual level, it may be hard for us to be sure that all actions driven by hate will have negative consequences, but everyone understands the immediate negative consequences of being filled with rage. Overcome with unpleasant feelings, out of control, you will see the faces of your friends and family darken with fear and defensiveness, your paranoia will be confirmed, and you will feel more justified in your surrender to hatred.

You may feel that your hate is a healthy reaction to an enemy. You may think it is a creative energy that enables you to remove obstacles to your happiness. Most insidious of all is that hate presents itself to you as your closest friend, even as your very self. When you hate someone or something, a voice inside that you identify as your own says, "That is just too much! I hate that! I can't stand it! I must not accept it! I will do something about it!" We obey that voice without question.

The first essential step in the yoga of cool heroism is the wisdom of understanding that none of the voices within our heads is intrinsically "ours." There are voices that we hear when we think, and we habitually identify them as familiar, as ours. When we search for the origins of these impulses to react the way we do, we find we have integrated the habits of those most familiar to us: our parents, our teachers, our friends, and our relatives. Those voices are nothing more than learned habits of thought. We can listen to them and follow them, or we can ignore them. We can cultivate another, critical voice, the voice of the Dharma, the voice of wisdom, and we can pick and choose which voice to listen to when we take action. We can gradually free ourselves of having to act compulsively when we hear "our own" inner voices telling us to hate, to fight, to retaliate.

We begin to become free of the compulsion to react automatically to other people when we see that enemies are created only by our perception that enemies prevent our happiness. But is that really possible? Through the meditation exercise in chapter 2, we discovered how little control external circumstances have on our peace of mind. It is our irritation and anxiety within that make the environment seem oppressive. When we are feeling good inside, calm and cheerful, even an objectively difficult situation seems manageable; and if we want to do something about it, we are more effective doing it calmly. It is the hate within us that creates our enemies, directly or indirectly. Once we are prone to hate and rage, we project around us a field of paranoia and all people become our potential enemies. We feel destructive toward them, and we assume they feel destructive toward us. When we become cool, we don't project enmity onto others; we can observe them more objectively, and if they are in fact out to cause trouble, we can quickly act to avoid it. The key insight is that hate itself is our worst enemy. It is not our energy, our instrument, or our tool. It deceives us into thinking we are it, and then *we* become *its* tool. In order to gain our freedom and happiness, to secure the happiness of those we care about, and to secure ourselves against aggression, we have to see through the masquerade of hate, see it as our real enemy, and begin a methodical campaign to conquer it.

The great adept Shantideva created an insightful guide to the way of life of the bodhisattva. His is a compelling program, a map and method, for overcoming hate and prejudice by developing empathy, tolerance, and wisdom. On the way to love, the true conquest of hate, you must reach the haven of unshakable tolerance.

First, you must come to the conclusion that anger and hate serve no useful purposes. Then you must deeply resolve to eliminate anger's ability to take control of you. Shantideva recommended that you focus your attention on the moment of discomfort that follows frustration: "My enemy hatred finds its fuel in the frustration of not getting what I want and of getting what I don't want; from there it grows and then destroys me. So I should totally eradicate the fuel of this enemy. Whatever happens to me, it shall not disturb my inner cheer."

We begin to gain control of hate by studying its pattern of arising as well as its immediate cause, which is mental discomfort—the uneasy feeling that grips us when either what we want is not taking place, or what we do not want is taking place. That frustration becomes uneasiness for a while, and then something snaps inside our minds: We feel unable to tolerate the stress of not having things the way we want them, and our frustration explodes into hate.

Frustration, since it arises from a tension between what is and what we want, can be dealt with in two ways. You can adapt your wants, or you can change what is. "Why be unhappy about something if I can do something about it? Why be unhappy about something if there's nothing I can do about it?" This idea is simple, but the advice is difficult to follow.

People tend to think the enlightened or spiritual thing to do is to swallow their emotions and let themselves be stepped on all the time. Often people won't say anything— they feel embarrassed as the heat rises in their throats; they flush and let it go by, only to lose control more violently later on. Nothing could be more wrong. When someone is doing something wrong to you, or not doing something truly important, step in at once. Say something firm about it. Call in help. Put a stop to it or get it going, as the case may be. Don't allow yourself to sit by getting frustrated, because you know it will eventually lead you to lose your cool. Cheerful assertiveness should be the attitude at such times.

For situations you have no ability to change, you might as well put your effort into reevaluating your internal reactions. It is more than likely that either you will see some new angles you can take advantage of and turn more to your liking, or after a while the situation itself will change. You will be able to remain cheerful if you can put the same energy into altering the inner scene as you would have put into changing the outer scene, had that been possible.

To develop cool heroism, start out by building up a tolerance for suffering, since hate is easily aroused by pain and injury. Then you must develop penetrating vision into the processes causing injury, to deconstruct any target of hatred you have created. Finally, you can cultivate a complete freedom from the urge to retaliate under any circumstances. Again, this does not mean that you don't ever act. It means that your action is an effective response arising out of wisdom and compassion, as opposed to a destructive and likely foolhardy reaction arising out of hate.

This discipline needs to be grounded in an awareness of the widespread predominance of suffering in the world. If you envision the great chain of life forming in the ocean of

evolution, you can reflect on the sufferings of all those beings. In particular, you can think about the suffering of
human life, the inevitability of bumping up against pain, injury, loss, and sorrow in the vast universe of time and space.
It is thus sensible to learn how better to tolerate the pain we
constantly feel, not to be so disturbed by it.

As we gradually develop a higher tolerance for suffering,
things that once seemed unbearable slowly become tolerable. Shantideva said, "There is nothing that does not become
easier through custom. Becoming accustomed to small
harms, I must patiently learn to tolerate greater harms."

Next, you reinforce this habituation with the cultivated
tolerance that is founded on awareness of reality. Your tolerance provides you with space between stimulus and your
reactions to the stimulus. You can use that space to look
more closely at the whole process of how you relate to people. You focus less on your own reactions and begin to see
others more clearly, more penetratingly. You can use the
power of critical wisdom to penetrate the superficial appearance of your antagonist and discern the deeper nature of
the situation.

The greatest spur to hate is the perception of a malicious
personality in the enemy, who seems willfully to choose to
harm us, to want us to feel pain, when really the antagonist
is most likely pursuing his or her own happiness. Though
we may bewail fate, we do not hate a sickness by thinking it
an evil demon. Instead, we see it as a mechanical process.

When we are seized by disturbing thoughts such as lust or hate, we may feel sickened, but we do not think of the afflicting thoughts themselves as intentionally wishing us ill. Rather than hate them, we think of them as mental mechanisms that take over our minds. But when we think of the enemy as a willful, intentional person with an evil design upon us, we lose control and hate him absolutely. We are swept away by hate, and our bodies, speech, and minds become its tools.

The way to reverse this helpless surrender to the blind, hot, destructive emotion is to realize that the "enemy" himself or herself is also being swept away by an irresistible negative inner force. He sees us as dangerous, as obstacles to his happiness; hate arises within him in a mechanical protective reaction, and he becomes the tool of that hate. If we see that, he becomes to us like a madman, dangerous and to be dealt with, but no longer the object of hate. There is nothing left to hate but hate itself. Shantideva says, in *Guide to the Bodhisattva Way of Life,* "Everything is governed by other factors, themselves governed by others; so nothing governs itself. Understanding this, I will not hate things that are nothing but hallucinatory apparitions." This realization enables us to begin to wield the energies of the situation and no longer be wielded *by* them, to regain control and make room for tolerance to develop.

The final step is to develop the tolerance of nonretaliation. This most powerful tolerance is the essential equipment of the cool bodhisattva hero or heroine. We begin to realize that we are our awareness and our tolerance. When we know that our awareness of reality cannot be destroyed and that tolerance fortifies our focus on that awareness, we can see any hardship, even the suffering of dying, as just a challenge that stimulates tolerance and awareness.

At that point you will have gained an invincible position, free of the involuntary response of violent defensiveness. You may intervene in a situation assertively and decisively, but your response will never be merely reactive. It will be proactive and much more effective. You will be immune to being carried away by emotion. And you will see clearly how much more you get from the exchange than the person who sees himself as your enemy and acts accordingly. His blindness cripples him, but it brings you the challenge to deepen your tolerance and equanimity.

The *Dhammapada* explains the Buddha's method in this enterprise in a famous couplet: "Not by hate does hatred come to an end. Only by love is hatred ended." Jesus said the same thing: "Love the Lord with all your heart, and your neighbor as yourself," and "Love your enemy." It is one thing to give these orders, but it is another to carry them out, as we all have discovered.

The attainment of such heights of transcendence and empathy may seem remote to us, but it is important for us to realize that many people have developed such tolerance and have discovered the strength that comes with it. We also can do it, and on the way, the more free we are from anger and the more tolerance we develop, the better we feel. Any degree of tolerance is its own reward.

The addiction to competitiveness is especially intense in our modern egalitarian societies, both communist and capitalist versions. We start with the ideal that all are equal, there is no royalty or hereditary nobility, and wind up with the belief that every individual has to be, have, do, and want everything, and if some have less than others, it is their own fault. Many cannot even watch an athlete in the Olympics without secretly thinking how they could have done it themselves if only they had tried, calming themselves only by the reminder that they can't do everything. Even the deities of our culture, the stars and celebrities, feel the wave of mass envy flow toward them, tainting the temporary and highly unstable flow of adulation.

How can we overcome our addiction to this pervasive competitiveness that allows us no rest, no ease, no contentment? We need to develop the ability to enjoy the happiness of others, to feel good about their successes. We must cultivate identification with others, empathize with them, and take delight in their good fortune. If we can sincerely wish one other person well (particularly someone close to us), we can create a wave of tolerance that can wash through an entire community.

To investigate and experience the essential equality of self and other, you have to begin by developing the armor of transcendent tolerance and the ability to use negative circumstances—losses, injuries, even death itself—as aids on the path. Only when freedom is so well grounded that nothing can disturb it is a person able to open up totally to others in universal empathy. From the firm ground of tolerance and impartiality, you can progress to the ability to leave your routine center of experience temporarily and enter another's heart, see through another's eyes, hear with another's ears, and feel another's feelings. When this ability becomes fluent, you can focus on empathizing with specific others, gaining deep insight into yourself, experiencing yourself as others do, learning viscerally which of your words and actions hurt others and which make them happy. This practice leads you beyond a narrow center of identity into a more fluid presence as a field of awareness, where relationships are gradually transformed from struggle to delight.

We can begin this meditation with one of Shantideva's formulas: "First of all I should strive to contemplate the equality of myself and others. I should cherish all beings as I do myself, as we all are equal in wanting pleasure, not wanting pain. . . . If my pain does not cause harm to others, only when I appropriate it as 'mine' does it become unbearable."*

---

*Translations modified from Thurman, *Essential Tibetan Buddhism* (San Francisco: HarperCollins, 1995); full translation available in Shan-

So, our first step is to understand that we all are equal in our pursuit of happiness and flight from suffering. Then, we use our critical thinking to explore the roots of our own suffering. We discover that suffering is not just an external event, a mere physical process, but that our experience of it is guided by a conception. In other words, we identify that personal, private suffering as "mine"; we appropriate it through the ego-process. Thus a warrior in the heat of battle or a person under hypnosis cannot feel pain that would be excruciating under normal circumstances, because his ego-appropriation is temporarily suspended. Our purpose in this meditation is not merely to reject ego-appropriation but to establish its expandability.

Shantideva's formula continues: "Likewise others' suffering does not affect me. Still, if I identify their pains as mine, they too become hard to bear." This is selflessness as compassion, the appropriation of all other beings as your own selfless self. All beings want happiness and do not want suffering, just like you. Our desires and our pains are no more or less serious than anyone else's. When we engage in this empathetic exchange, the enormity of our "own" suffering becomes less intense.

It may seem unrealistic for us to think that anything practical comes from imagining a pain we do not feel. But we do

tideva, *Guide to Bodhisattva Way of Life* (Dharamsala, India: Library of Tibetan Works and Archives, 1981).

this all the time when we act to avoid future pain: getting out of the way of an oncoming car; cranking up the fan in summer. Since we can expand our protective concern to cover our future selves—beings other than our presently existing selves—surely we can expand it to include other beings existing in the present. We do so already when we identify with tribes, nations, races, or faiths. The "we" can become powerful enough to override instincts of self-preservation, such as when individuals willingly die in battles or as martyrs to their faith. Why, then, can't we use the "bodhisattva reconditioning" to stretch our sense of identity to include all beings, so that we see others as limbs on the single body of life?

Our distinction between suffering which we are concerned about and suffering we ignore is arbitrarily delineated. Just as one alleviates one's own suffering for no other reason than that it hurts, so should one alleviate that of others just because it hurts them. It is easy, then, to see why a person with such an expanded basis of self-identification, one whose self-identification no longer excludes "others," could easily undergo suffering in the one immediate self to alleviate much greater sufferings on the part of the many selves. "Having seen the flaws in cherishing myself," says Shantideva, "and the ocean of good in cherishing others, I shall completely abandon all self-concern and cultivate concern for others. And just as I protect myself from unpleasant things, however small, so should I protect others with a compassionate and caring mind."

No righteous pride arises from altruism cultivated on

such insight, just as we do not congratulate ourselves for our kindness when we feed ourselves. We just do it naturally. The psychology of the bodhisattva is nothing otherworldly; it is not too far beyond the normal call of human beings. In fact, it is evident from experience that we are never happier than when we lose the confinement of the narrow, habitual ego-sense, to whatever degree. Actually, we are happy when we are free of wanting to be happy. *Wanting* to be happy automatically makes us unhappily aware of lack. In Shantideva's words, "Whatever joy there is in this world, all comes from wanting others to be happy; and whatever suffering there is in this world, all comes from wanting oneself to be happy." So, if we want to be happy, we can stop worrying about being happy and focus instead on wanting others to be happy. This urge leads us to try to care for others fully, knowing that they will be happy only when they stop yearning to be happy.

Our next step on the bodhisattva path is to practice the exchange of self and others, first in meditation and then in action. Imagine yourself to be someone you know whom you usually consider inferior to yourself in some respect, someone who tends to feel jealous of you. Then, look at yourself from the eyes of that person and concentrate on feeling sharp jealousy toward yourself. It is startling how you look to yourself when you see with jealous eyes.

Continue by imagining yourself as another person whom you usually think of as your equal. Then, look back at yourself through their eyes with feelings of rivalry and competitiveness. Finally, imagine yourself as someone who usually seems superior to you in some respect, and look back at yourself with condescension or contempt. Such meditations can be powerful tools for widening your view and appreciating others' perspectives.

In all of these practices, wisdom combines with compassion to generate the great universal, unconditional compassion. That universal compassion does not perceive any particular object of its encompassing empathy, hence it automatically perceives beings into liberation—it *sees* them into freedom.

This luminous soul is described in Buddhist texts as fine gold that never tarnishes, a new moon ever on the increase, a fire that grows ever more intense, an inexhaustible treasury for others' prosperity, an ocean unruffled by winds of complications, an immovable king of mountains, a miracle medicine, the greatest friend, a fountain pouring forth undiminished the meaning of the liberating truth, and a great cloud from which rains the source of life and wealth of all beings.

The messianic drive of universal responsibility is hollow unless accompanied by careful focus on the emotional reality of responding to individual others. As one Tibetan lama used to say, "Don't be like those bodhisattvas who constantly vow to save all living beings but can't seem to get along with the people they see every day." It's one thing to develop the power of patience as an individual, but how are these messianic principles manifested in a society full of nonenlightened people?

The detailed counsel we've explored thus far provides a framework on which to organize guidelines for enlightened social action in modern times. Everyone can apply these principles in his or her own sphere of activity; political parties can be formed with such principles in their platforms; and enlightened communities and individuals can work to spread such principles and attitudes.

We should think of Nagarjuna's advice to King Udayi as applicable to our modern situation as well. Good advice is often unpleasant to people when they first hear it, especially to rich and powerful kings who are used to being flattered and to having their own way. Not only governors and industrial chiefs, but the entire populations of the developed countries are in a way full of people of royal powers, used to consuming what we want, being flattered and waited upon. We are accustomed to having unpleasantly realistic things such as corpses, sickness, madness, and poverty kept out of our sight. We do not want to hear that all is impermanent, that unenlightened life is essentially painful and impure. We do not want to acknowledge that all beings are the equals of ourselves and those we love. We do not want to hear that there is no absolute self and no absolute property and no absolute right. The hundreds of millions of "kings" and "queens" living in the developed world must face their obligations to other peoples, to other species, and to nature itself.

The wealth of modern nations comes from three main sources. First is the generosity of hard work, self-sacrifice, and inventiveness of earlier generations. Capitalism itself is, in its essence, not a matter of hoarding and attachment, but a matter of ascetic self-restraint in consumption and of the investment of wealth. The more that is given up from present consumption to productive investment, the more that is available for future consumption. Those who simply consume and hoard soon lose their wealth. It is a fact not only of karmic evolution but also of stable economics that the basis of wealth is self-restraint and generosity.

Second is the generosity of older, gentler nations from whose Asian, African, and American lands enormous wealth has been and still is being extracted by entrepreneurs.

The third source of modern wealth is the generosity of the earth herself. We can repay former generations with our generosity toward future generations, by investing in their future, and by restraining our consumption. We can repay the heirs of the exploited by giving back some of the fruits of the wealth they let our ancestors take, especially in the form of equipment they need to produce more wealth themselves. And we can repay the earth by ceasing to pollute her, cleaning up the enormous messes we have made and investing in her long-term health. We still have the chance to make these gifts voluntarily. If we fail to take that chance, all inevitably will be lost. Nagarjuna encourages us: "Always be of magnanimous mind, delighting in magnificent deeds. Magnanimous actions bring forth magnificent fruits."

Petty-mindedness, scarcity psychology, short-term profit-seeking, destructive rapacity—these are the real enemies. Their opposite is magnanimity, which makes all people friends. Transcendence is the root of generosity. Generosity is the root of evolutionary progress. Evolutionary progress eventually provides access to freedom for the bliss of transcendence. These three qualities form a golden braid, creating a lifestyle conducive to peace.

Nagarjuna considered it obvious that the king is obligated to care for all people in the whole nation as if they were his children. In modern terms, both the welfare system created by Franklin D. Roosevelt in the United States, and the welfare socialism the western European states implemented fit extremely well with this policy. But recently there has been a growing belief that while any reasonable person would like to give everything to everyone, it is bad for people to get goods for nothing and, further, there is not enough wealth to support everyone. The assumptions underlying this antiwelfare reaction we see around the world are that people are inherently lazy and deserve their fates, and that wealth is inherently insufficient.

Certainly such attitudes were present already in Nagarjuna's day and earlier. A popular former-life story of the Buddha illustrates this paradox of generosity and wealth: Everyone loved Prince Vessantara because he gave everyone everything he or she asked for. Yet his nation came to fear him when it seemed he would give away even the very sources of its wealth. So the people shrank back in fright, clutched what they had to themselves, and banished their real source of joy, the generous prince.

Since the welfare system was installed in the United

States, the country has produced the greatest wealth ever by any nation in history, and this in the midst of a series of disastrous wars, with aftermaths during which America gave enormous treasure to rebuild the nations it had defeated. Now, the rulers of America think that the gifts to the people, which have been the real source of their optimism, the real energy behind their productivity, are exhausting them, and so they want to take it all away. In this confused effort to clutch at what they see as scarce and shrinking wealth, citizens and leaders of our prosperous nations are destroying the source of that wealth, their own love, optimistic confidence, and educated creativity.

Nagarjuna's counsels to King Udayi provide us with an antidote to this downward spiral, pointing the way to an individualistic, nonviolent, education-oriented, altruistic society, decentralized yet global. His program of self-cultivation, especially of the critical wisdom necessary for understanding selflessness and propertylessness; the detachment needed to question the desirability of excessive passions; the universalistic love that extends the opportunity for happiness to all through education aimed at enlightenment; and the generous compassion dedicated to providing everyone with everything to satisfy their basic needs so that they may have leisure to consider their higher aims and opportunities is as relevant to us today as it was for King Udayi.

Chapter 7

THE
WORLD-TAMING
ADEPTS

*I*f we lack a special art, the skeptic's sense that empathy makes one more miserable seems to be correct. We already feel our own pain and are powerless do much about it. How much worse it is to feel the pains of others and be helpless to do anything for them. But when one makes the commitment to attain enlightenment for the benefit of all, a compassionate energy is released and the artistry for living transforms immediate relationships from struggle into loving play. As our empathy and love flow out to embrace all living beings on earth, the galaxies, and beyond, we come up against not only black holes of despair but also vast suns of confidence and determination. By becoming a being of radiant blissfulness, a bodhisattva is a living instrument that can effectively bring about the aim of all true love—the happiness of infinite beloved others. This goodwill moves to tame the whole society, the whole world, even the universe so that it becomes a place in which the maximum number of people can attain the highest level of happiness. Since the universe is infinite, containing infinite beings in infinite universes within it, that will becomes a kind of messianic madness that explodes in the form of a vow to create a universe that itself works to liberate souls—a buddhaland or buddhaverse.

Messianic madness by itself is exhausting unless it is balanced by the wisdom that understands the absolute unreality of all conventional things. As mad with universal responsibility as I may be, I cannot get anything done without changing myself, without freeing myself from routinized imagination and becoming a buddha myself. Then, I can create a world of love. I can create a mandala, a "soul-perfecting circle," a perfected environment wherein life itself is revealed as a process of transmutation of suffering into bliss.

It was in the second half of the first millennium c.e. when the enlightenment movement, which had always maintained the value of the individual, clearly took a new turn. A new breed of spiritual heroes and heroines arose in India, the world-transforming mahasiddhas, or great adepts.

These great adepts, whether kings or washermen, began as people who had reached a point in their evolutionary progress where they were excruciatingly aware of the priceless opportunity of a human lifetime. They were intelligent enough to know that a life lived just for the sake of eating, working, procreating, and seeking sense pleasures is a waste of time. (Several of the adepts attracted their teachers by spending their time lamenting their useless lives, wishing for access to a higher meaning, a way of life sure to have some meaningful fruition.)

Finally, they became so mad with compassion that they were no longer able to plod along for incalculable eons of ordinary history until full enlightenment. They could not stand to wait so long to become able to do something about the horrible sufferings of all beings, all their mothers. They sought to attain buddhahood in the immediate context of this life. The Buddha is said to have manifested in special male and female forms to teach such urgent bodhisattvas the esoteric Tantric Vehicle or Diamond Vehicle, the technological or apocalyptic vehicle of immediate revelation and immediate transformation.

Tantric practice begins when the bodhisattva, after being initiated by a great master—a process of consecration whereby the bodhisattva is anointed with the healing elixirs of the enlightened imagination—abandons the "gross" world of the physical senses and their objects and enters a dreamlike, magical, and extremely subtle realm where eons can be moments, universes are contained within atoms, and this universe is an atom of a larger universe. The initiation itself provides the doorway from the ordinary world to the world structured by enlightened beings. It is at this level that the bodhisattva adopts the mahasiddha ideal and is empowered to visualize, through sustained concentration guided by a detailed sacred architectural plan and a detailed divine anatomy, the environment as a perfect crystal palace with majestic gardens; the time as the golden age of total fulfillment; his or her own body as the jewel body that perfectly articulates all the highest qualities of enlightened love, compassion, joy; his or her companions as perfect heroes and heroines already established in enlightenment; and his or her self as the diamond of the buddhamind that is perfectly aware of selflessness as the clear light of the void.

This enjoyment of mandalic reality is so secure that the practitioner perceives death as a luminous, sustaining foundation rather than a lurking doom; perceives the after-death dreamlike transformation as a bliss immersion rather than a wild flight or a dizzying fall; and perceives all life experiences as aesthetic experience of the highest creativity—every movement, every gesture, every word, every thought, every breath a work of art communicating freedom and happiness to all beings. The practitioner has mastered this process of creative visualization when he or she can enter at will this extraordinary subjectivity and dwell within it as long as desired, exiting at will to interact with beings in the ordinary environment. It culminates with the practitioner's becoming able to achieve a completely secure experience of him- or herself as a buddha, filled with bliss and wisdom in a heavenly mansion, whose radiance enfolds the universe and all beings into their own highest evolutionary state.

This is not to say that enlightenment is merely a sustained

work of imagination, that the adept imagines his or her way to buddhahood, so to speak. When the adept masters this process of creative visualization, he or she begins the perfection process, the process through which what is imagined becomes reality. The creation process is the targeting procedure that directs the extraordinary mission to the goal. In the perfection process, the mission actually begins.

At this point, extremely subtle minds and bodies are introduced. The sacred architecture of the environment and the divine biology of the coarse body, with its many faces, arms, legs, and ornaments all expressing the faculties and experiences of enlightenment, are complemented by a spiritual genetic engineering, wherein spiritual experiences are reduced to the movement of genes and inner energies within a subtle central nervous system. The practices begin to act as an immune system of the psyche, aiding the practitioner to swiftly conquer the demons of the unconscious. Through this refinement of the subjectivity to a subtle awareness, transitional states of bliss and dissolution can be experienced in a much finer grain, or at a much higher magnification, or in a much slowed motion, in order to preserve the continuity of awareness and maintain stability of control over the deepest processes of life, ecstasy, and death. The journey is arduous and dangerous. More than death-defying, it is death-conquering in that it embraces death, practices death, and uses the processes of death to achieve complete immunity to all compulsions, including death.

The tantric exercise of mandala creation is a rehearsal on an intimate scale for universe rebuilding. The bodhisattva vows to create a buddhaverse, a world that expresses to others the wisdom, compassion, and love of his or her complete enlightenment. It is extremely difficult even to imagine how to create this kind of environment. Think of how much knowledge is required to make a greenhouse so that plants can flourish optimally. What would you have to know to make a greenhouse buddhaverse for living beings in which they all could flourish optimally? An architect tries to imagine the residents of his or her building living a certain lifestyle, doing a certain work. The architect visualizes spaces and volumes and forms of subliminal influence that will create an environment that will bring out the best in these imagined residents. The practice of mandala creation is a playful rehearsal for the creation of the best of all possible worlds.

As India reached its inner consummation and fruition, the seeds of its blossom were carried out by these adept individuals, conquistadors for enlightenment civilization, to the wider world. At the same time, the bees of greedy and aggressive societies of frustrated and hence warlike people homed in on India's luscious blossom, loaded with the pollen of beauty, wealth, knowledge, and access to individual freedom. India's growth proceeded thus: It exported its enlightened lifestyle through individual adepts while it absorbed the invasions of unenlightened hordes coming from

Iran, Central Asia, and eventually Europe, who suppressed the overt institutions and symbols of that lifestyle, bringing a return of violence.

The great adepts of India, along with numerous merchants and sailors and other adventurers, traveled all over Southeast and East Asia, as well as Iran, Arabia, Egypt, and the Mediterranean. Everywhere they went during the first millennium, they had a profound impact. Sri Lanka was transformed from a cannibal isle to an enlightenment-oriented society in a few centuries. The jungle tribes of Southeast Asia gradually became interested in the higher purpose of human life and moderated somewhat their vicious jungle wars, taking time off to build temples and monasteries, ordain monks and nuns, support mass education in the enlightenment teachings, and generally try to calm down their violent cultures. The Indonesians and Malays were turned bit by bit toward enlightenment. The Chinese, Koreans, and Japanese gradually integrated the enlightenment civilization into their highly structured, authoritarian societies. Several dynasties in Iran and the many kingdoms of Central Asia supported the enlightenment movement. And the many missions in Ashoka's era to Egypt, Mesopotamia, Syria, Palestine, Turkey, and even Greece had undoubted impact, though it is sometimes hard to discern because of the strong ethnocentrism of later European historians. Even after the Islamic sweep of Asia, the adepts introduced their arts into the lineages of Sufism, which fed back throughout the entire militaristic structure of the Muslim empires.

The story of Ghantapa and his accomplished consort is an example of the rampant individualism of the adepts. Ghantapa had mastered most of the stages of the path as a monk and bodhisattva scholar in central India. He was known as a great holy man, though he felt he could no longer progress within the conventional institutions quickly enough to aid other beings. Individualism had become highly appreciated in all the Indian kingdoms by that time, so he wandered to the east, into the territories of the Pala kings of present-day Bengal. A wanderer in search of absolute truth and alternative realities could always find sustenance from a supportive populace. In fact, the people would vie with one another to feed and serve such holy beings.

As Ghantapa's saintly reputation spread within the Pala kingdom, the king himself sought to serve Ghantapa food and drink with his own royal hands, perhaps intending to become his patron and install him as a sage, an ornament to the court. Ghantapa turned his bowl upside down, saying, "I would never accept support from a corrupt ruler such as Your Majesty." The king withdrew in a fury, vowing to prove who was holy and who corrupt. He posted a huge reward for any woman who could seduce the ascetic. After some time, a courtesan came forward, proclaiming that her sixteen-year-old daughter would not fail to effect the downfall of the holy man. The courtesan began to send her servants to

Ghantapa's hut with food. Her daughter would accompany them demurely as their mistress, witness Ghantapa's acceptance of the meal, and then leave with the servants. Bit by bit, the beautiful maiden shot the arrows of passion into Ghantapa's heart with the delicate flourish of her garment, the arch of her eyebrow, the flutter of her lash, the humble bowing of her neck—all the exquisite subtle graces the Indian arts of love had so fully developed by that era. But she made no obvious move and simply continued to see to the bringing of the food.

One day when the old courtesan mother thought the time was ripe, the daily meal was not delivered at the usual time, and Ghantapa went out in the afternoon to beg his food. When he returned to his hut, the evening had turned stormy and he discovered the young maiden sitting alone inside the hut with a delicious meal. He was embarrassed and, after taking a bit of the food, asked her to withdraw. She politely refused, reminding him that the road home would be dangerous in the storm. It was not long before they fell into each other's arms. The holy man became an ex-monk, an impassioned lover, and she his consort. She left her mother's house, and they began to live together openly.

When the king heard this news, he was delighted. He would have marched to the hut immediately, but the old courtesan asked him to be patient, as there was still no absolute proof of Ghantapa's downfall. The loving couple lived in bliss for several years and even had a child. But finally, the courtesan claimed her reward and the king and all the members of the court went off in grand procession to confront the corrupted monk and savor their triumph.

When the entourage met the couple in front of the hut, the lovers were holding hands. The child was in Ghantapa's free hand, and a bottle of wine was in the consort's. The king crowed, "Now, who is corrupt and who is pure?" Ghantapa said, "There is nothing impure here." He raised the child in the air, and it transformed into a shining vajra-scepter, a symbol of the magic body of enlightenment. The consort threw down the wine bottle, and it transformed into a matching vajra-bell, a symbol of the clear-light transparency of enlightenment.

The couple floated up into the sky stark naked. They expanded to superhuman size, entwined themselves into a yogic sexual union, and radiated dazzling rainbow light. They were immediately recognized as the archetypal great adept buddhaform, Chakrasamvara, the Supreme Bliss buddha-couple.

Perhaps the most successful direction the great adepts took their enlightenment technology was north into the Himalayas, to Tibet, where it gradually rooted and eventually bore tremendous fruit, transforming that bellicose society into a mandala of the peaceful, perfected universe—not a fully realized mandala, but a nationwide dedication to bringing it into being.

Padma Sambhava was the great adept who in the eighth century C.E. tamed warlike Tibet. Padma Sambhava means "Lotus-born," since, according to legend, he was born miraculously on a lotus in a lake in answer to the prayers and threats of the heirless king of Oddiyana, an ancient kingdom encompassing northern Pakistan and Afghanistan.

Like Shakyamuni before him, Padma ran away from his duty as prince of Oddiyana early on, became a monk, and later an adept who operated outside the conventions of the monasteries, trying unconventional means for achieving enlightenment quickly, as he could no longer bear the suffering of other beings. He began living in caves and charnel grounds, conquering demons, developing his abilities to confront the nature of reality. He developed a following and later went to the Pala kingdom, where he found his consort, the princess Mandarava. As was common with female adepts, she was in deep trouble for having disobeyed her father, the king, by refusing a marriage of state. Padma saved her, and the two began a meditation practice that involved yogic sexual union. When they were noticed by the public in their flamboyant coupling, the father was so furious that he had them fastened to a giant pyre that burned for three days and nights. When the fire was spent, the couple was found still in blissful union, undisturbed by the flames, nestled on a giant lotus in the midst of a sandalwood-scented lake that had sprung up on the site of the pyre.

This resurrection overwhelmed the king and the citizens both aesthetically and metaphysically. Padma and Mandarava gave many teachings to the entire nation on tolerance, wisdom, and compassion before heading for the Himalayas to continue their blissful yoga.

Toward the end of the eighth century C.E., the great philosopher Shantarakshita, abbot of the greatest Indian monastic universities, was invited by the emperor of Tibet to come to that militaristic Himalayan land and build the first monastic university there. Emperor and abbot labored mightily, but the local shamans were dead set against the enlightenment principles. Their tribal deities thought it offensive, for it would deny them their traditional blood sacrifices, and the warrior nobility could think of nothing more useless than a population of nonviolent monks who did nothing but eat, sleep, study, and meditate. The abbot made an architectural plan, and the emperor engaged artisans and laborers to raise the walls of the complex. But every night the tribal deities came with ogre workers and took the walls down. Soon the treasury was near exhaustion. A plague broke out, and the shamans blamed the monastery-building for offending the gods. The abbot advised the emperor to send a mission to India to invite the great adept Padma Sambhava, for he alone had the ability to face down the shamans and the tribal deities and demons.

Padma was waiting for the embassy at the border and agreed to accompany them back to Tibet. When he met the emperor, he enraged the courtiers by refusing to bow to him. They knew that monks did not bow to laymen, not even to kings, but Padma was not now a monk. "Who do you think you are, that you do not bow to the emperor of all Inner Asia?" "Who do you think I am, that you do not bow to me, the emperor of the Dharma?" was the prompt retort. Padma made an elegant sweeping gesture toward the crowd with his arm, and his fingertips became flamethrowers. The emperor and nobles ducked, involuntarily bowing to the great adept, who smiled, having made his point in a way immediately understandable to military men.

The adept's principle is to teach the deities of a nation first so that the people will be easier to handle. Padma went up onto the sandy, low Hebo mountain, overlooking the great river across from the Tsetang mountain, where the first Tibetans were said to have been born from the union of an angelic monkey and an earthy ogress. On that mountain he went into retreat, after instructing the emperor to stay away until invited. Thunder, lightning, and ominous portents surrounded the mountain during the months that followed.

Eventually the emperor became impatient and went up to the mountain during a frightful storm. He did not see Padma, but walked into a mammoth struggle between a giant eagle and a ferocious dragon, on the order of Godzilla vs. Mothra with cinematic special effects. The eagle was in the process of swallowing the dragon whole, only a bit of tail still thrashing from its mouth. When the frightened emperor cried out, the great beasts ceased the struggle and began to fade. The dragon became a small serpent and slithered away, and the eagle reverted to the form of Padma Sambhava. Padma was furious. He scolded the emperor for his impatience and predicted that the dragon serpent, a manifestation of the ego of the national deity of Tibet, was now only incompletely tamed. While the emperor could proceed to build the monastic university, the deities could not be relied upon indefinitely. They would eventually withdraw their support for the enlightenment movement, and a terrible price would have to be paid.

The building project was swiftly completed. Shantarakshita returned along with other expert Indian masters, they ordained the first batch of Tibetan monk-scholars, and Samyey University opened its doors. For the next half century, thousands of learned scholars from all over Asia assembled there, bringing with them texts and knowledge of all the arts and sciences of the day in one of the great cross-cultural transmissions and acts of preservation in world history. Soon after the universal vehicle and tantric teachings were brought to Tibet, they would be nearly eradicated from India, their place of birth.

Padma went on to make Tibet a safe zone for enlightenment. He selected a group of twenty-five disciples of special ability, some women but mostly men, and withdrew from the scholarly work of the university to the crystal caves in the surrounding mountains. There he transmitted to these twenty-five great adepts a feast of esoteric teachings. They all had the exceptional ability to understand these immediately, swiftly put them into practice, and soon attained high realizations. They then spread out around Tibet and extended Padma's work of taming the many tribal deities living in the trans-Himalayan mountain fastnesses. While the monks and scholars at the new university labored to create a new civilization for Tibet, these masters worked directly with the natural forces of the land, the national unconscious, transforming them from bloodthirsty savage deities into servants of the Dharma.

Having completed the foundation of this special Dharma treasury in Tibet and having mystically installed a high-altitude mandala of radiant spiritual energy there, Padma departed to tame other savage lands. In legend, he still lives on in his hidden paradise somewhere in the jungles of Africa. And the Tibetan people carried on his peaceful legacy until the Communists invaded in 1950.

Each of the great adepts has a similar story. They show the individual human being standing out in complete fulfillment in all his or her glory, overwhelming the collective and its conventional routines. They always triumph over the confusion and negativity of society and manifest an inspiration to that society, thus making room for the fulfillment of the society's individuals. These great adepts are the supreme artists of life. They themselves are their own masterpieces. They have taken the materials of their own ordinary bodies, speech, and minds, and they have transformed them into exalting works of art. When their contemporaries encounter these works, at first they are shocked, scandalized, frightened, and angered. But then the sheer bliss and beauty of them overwhelm their rigid attitudes, lift them out of their habitual selves, and flood their sensibilities with an unimagined joy and fulfillment. The political impact of such demonstrations of the power of individualism is immense. It is the force of transcendentalism becoming socially and aesthetically palpable to the whole citizenry. This is what Padma Sambhava was up to in Tibet when he pacified that violent society, and what Ghantapa was manifesting to the court when he and his consort revealed the power of their pure nature.

The existence of the great adepts is the proof of the positive development of ancient Indian society and of creative individualism as the fruit of enlightenment practice. Unconcerned with any institutional identity, they were regarded as outstanding exemplars by all traditions of the day, numbered as "The Eighty Four" by the Buddhists and as "The Eighty" by the Hindus. These iconoclasts were the Indian forerunners of the Zen masters of East Asia, of the nineteenth-century Romantic poets, and of American individualists such as Walt Whitman and Allen Ginsberg. They embodied the full potential of life. They were the psychonauts, the leading experimenters of the inner technologies of enlightenment civilization, just as modern astronauts are the leading explorers of our outer technologies. The female and

male great adepts found in their inner universes the resources to triumph over sorrow and inadequacy in order to
bring joy and hope to people everywhere.

When we encounter the world of these psychonaut adepts,
we recoil from the scent of magic, from the joke of the supernatural, from the fantasy of the mystical, from the concept of a high technology of the mind. Yet when we come to
materialistic high technology, no fantasy is too extravagant.
We proudly extol the wonders of modern science and technology. We chuckle over how our own ancestors would have
seen a picture on a television set as a product of witchcraft.
How they would have thought the view of the microcellular
world through an electron microscope was an alien glimpse
of hell. How a rocket to the moon would have been condemned as violating the realm of the angels. How gene splic-
ing would be a Frankensteinian tinkering with God's
creation. And how the obliteration of all life on earth by
hundreds of thousands of atomic and hydrogen bombs was a
diabolical and ridiculous proposition. We have learned to
accept all these wonders as normal, everyday realities. And
yet we seize our present sense of how things are just as
rigidly as did the medievals their sense of the flatness of the
earth.

The enlightenment tradition discovered the micro and
macro dimensions more than two thousand years ago by

using sophisticated contemplative practices to augment the sixth mental sense of inner vision. They discovered the infinite divisibility of the atom. They discovered microbes. And, most important to the pursuit of enlightenment, they discovered their own neurons and even the subatomic level of their own awareness. This realm is supernatural only in relation to a constricted definition of natural. It is mystical only when its analytic investigation is not completed. It is magic only when the technique involved is not understood.

Our minds perform magic all the time. When you see an item in your visual field, your brain has shuffled through the data bank stored in its neurons and has sent up a percept, a particular pattern stored in a set of these neurons. It has filtered through its rod and cone neurons the incoming photons reflected off all the objects in the visual field. It has organized a patch according to color and distance in relation to a foreground and a background. It has selected a group to distinguish; it has matched them with the synaptic percept pattern; and, lo and behold, we see a "tree," or a "house," or a "lake." This process is very like a software program directing a computer to produce a picture of a tree in response to our typing the word "tree" on the keyboard. Such a program is a very complex patterning structure, operating within a complex system. Now, if the software developed a virus, if it produced a car picture when we typed "tree," we would use another sort of software, a diagnostic utility program, which would enter into the software structure itself and look for a gap or a glitch. This program would have no idea of "tree" or "car" but would be looking through the binary switches within the system for a problem. It would be looking for a deficient microentity with a microentity subjectivity. Having reduced the car image to a blizzard of digital dots, it would look for the controller of the misperception that caused the car dots to be triggered by the "tree" command.

This diagnostic utility program functions like our sixth sense, the mental sense. It works within the structuring patterns that control the computer's attention to its input and output channels, which are comparable to the five senses of the ordinary person. It is a kind of subtle awareness that operates from the binary ground level of the machine. Enlightenment scientists have developed such an awareness through contemplation, systematic analysis, and penetration of coarse structures. They can perceive photons directly from the neuron level; they can detach subjectivity from structured coarse perception and exercise it from the more subtle levels. With this specially developed mental sense, they can grasp and transform reality in unprecedented ways.

During the European Enlightenment, Voltaire ridiculed the notion that this world is the best of all possible worlds, a notion that the Jewish or Christian monotheist is forced to wrestle with because of his or her belief in the existence of an omnipotent, all-compassionate Creator. Voltaire sent poor

Candide through misery after misery, having him stubbornly repeat, "It's the best of all possible worlds!" after every disaster.

The Enlightenment thinkers of that time were tired of the Church rationalizing everything bad that happened in the world as being for the best. If God is all-good and all-powerful, then He has no need to create creatures who suffer. If we therefore seem to suffer, it is by His design as an educational experience.

Voltaire thought that swallowing this rationalization of suffering and evil crippled human beings, making them slaves to the Church, to their political masters, and to tradition. It made them unable to think for themselves, to take their destinies into their own hands, to intervene in the world to ameliorate their own situations. So he ridiculed Candide to help Europeans have the courage to rely on their own reason. And Europeans responded by developing science and technology: They developed industry and intervened radically in the processes of nature; they challenged taboos, secularized everything, and gained enormous new knowledge of the physical sciences; they set out to transform nature, and they succeeded to a very great degree. When traditional social structures got in their way, they overthrew them in the great series of revolutions that is still sweeping the world. When lack of wealth got in their way, they invented better weapons and travel technology and proceeded to subjugate all nations and races who did not share their science, power of travel, or warfare. They conquered the world.

From the seventeenth century until the twentieth century, Westerners thought this was working out. We came into the twentieth century thinking capitalism or communism or bureaucracy, armed with science and technology, was about to create utopia, a heaven on earth, with freedom from disease, freedom from want and poverty, freedom from suffering. We were on the brink of making the best of all possible worlds out of stainless steel, plastics, chemicals, social systems, universities, and corporations.

But it hasn't worked. Some of us have sunk into confirmed nihilism and are waiting for pollution, population, war, and impoverishment to obliterate all life on earth. Others have reverted to old Candide-like attitudes and are sitting back, waiting for a savior.

The world is neither best nor worst—in an objective sense, the world is what the individual makes it. A world of individuals is the intersubjective, collective mind field of all those individuals. Standing on the ground of freedom, we can see things afresh, enter relationships renewed and with a new purpose of sharing freedom and happiness. We can become poets and seers of reality. We can become great adepts, true individuals, agents of compassion. To live in a world is to be constantly creating that world. To live in a nation requires the knowledge to understand the nightmares and dreams of one's ancestors, the vision to dream of something better, and the courage to realize that better dream.

For an adept to awaken the messianic impulse within a particular nation, the world-rebuilding must be based on the world picture of that nation. The nation has its gods, its myths, its founding heroes and heroines, its ideals, and its sense of mission in the world, just like an individual. The adept must first study the culture like an anthropologist and then fit in with that world picture, fulfill its ideals, and in some sense align with its myths. But the messianic adept cannot just fit in. He or she also must transform the culture, graft the new enlightenment-oriented shoots onto the old traditions.

We have imagined our world to be tamed, or civilized, since we live in cities and seem to have nature under control. It is hard for us to think of ourselves as wild and untamed. But "civilized" should mean something more than just living in cities. It should mean that we are wise, gentle, just, and even artistic in our dealings with the world and with other animals and humans. Our civilization is what I call an "outer civilization"; its modernity is an outer modernity. It is based on turning the full force of human reason on the enterprise of conquering and taming the outer universe—the universe of matter and energy, lands and continents, materials and products—and on viewing people as resources to be managed and developed for production. In the sense of being able to destroy things on a planetary scale, we have some power over nature—short of controlling major planetary phenomena, such as tectonic-plate movement, volcanoes, hurricanes, and so forth. Our creative power falls short, too, and we have found that we cannot fashion the pure land of materialism, the utopia of the capitalists and Communists, where people as bodies with interchangeable parts can be kept alive forever; where everyone can have a car; where population, resources, food, and wealth all are kept in perfect balance with no serious want; where all natural discomfort is controlled and moderated.

And what have we not controlled? We have not tamed our own minds very much at all. Our religions did do something of a taming job up until the modern period. They kept our world picture wholesome and made it meaningful for us to restrain our more bestial impulses most of the time. But they did not provide anyone, except a small monastic and mystical elite, with the methodology to overcome the negative instincts once and for all. And so, when the suppressive power of ideology, church, and state could no longer keep our inner nature in check, out it burst in all its violent glory, in fascism, in destructive orgies of technological warfare, and in the planetary terrorism of mutually assured nuclear destruction.

We are the savages of outer modernity. We have reached the point where the lethal passions are emerging as planetary enemy number one. Meanwhile the great adepts have been quietly turning their attention toward us for several centuries. We do not notice their efforts on a social scale. We might, as individuals, learn a little meditation or visit a Zen center or a Tibetan monastery. But we do not expect these institutions or teachers to have any significant social impact.

We do not see this as having a political impact, because we do not think anything can be done. We are certain that our sense of utter helplessness is realistic and appropriate.

The middle way between the two extremes of authoritarian repression and self-defeating nihilism is to take our systematic and scientific cleverness, enthusiasm, and ingenuity and turn our attention toward the inner self the way we have turned it so successfully on outer nature. Why not engineer spiritual balance and harmony? We can investigate the lethal passions and their instinctual foundations, find out precisely how they work, how they take hold of us and use us as their instruments. Then we can devise technologies and arts to conquer them and to transmute them into useful energies. Or we can use the technologies of the adepts who have gone before.

In Tibet, where the enlightenment tradition flourished for a thousand years, guided by the great adepts, Padma Sambhava is a universal hero of culture transformation. He stood up to the potent father deity in their epic confrontation on the mountain and swallowed him into the eagle's belly of his transcendent wisdom. No matter how great and powerful the deity, the infinity perspective of voidness dwarfed him into insignificance. The security of being great became nothing, he encountered his impermanence, and he felt himself dissolve and die. Padma gave him a crash course in his actuality of selflessness. At the same time the deity experienced humbling disillusionment, he attained relief from the beginningless misconception of the separateness of all things. What was interrupted on Mount Hebo by the frightened and impatient emperor was probably the relief and joy that is the second instant of the enlightenment, following upon the total letting go into wisdom. As a result, the dragon once more lashed its tail a few decades later, rising in egocentric anger and persecuting the nascent enlightenment civilization.

This total reformation is the work of the anthropologist great adept. It is a psychic diving into the archetypal plane of a nation's collective unconscious, where the mythic patterns of the national ego dwell. There the adept must fight with the local gods, a battle he wins through his special wisdom of selflessness. It is not a case of two ego powers confronting each other, as when one culture invades another. Rather, it is a case of the adept being able to turn the deity's strength against him. The adept, through his or her wisdom of selflessness, is always himself and the other at the same time. He experiences the battle from the enemy's viewpoint as well as his own. He anticipates the god's every move, because it is simultaneously his move, drawing out the deity's greatest terrors, since he also feels them. The gods put out their ultimately wrathful manifestations and instantaneously see them coming back at them, magnified a millionfold. A god who is used to smashing whole universes into hells with his tiniest whiff of righteous wrath suddenly feels countless wrathful forces crashing down upon himself, bent back by voidness's space/time singularity warp. The black hole of Padma's selfless wisdom sucks all negative energy into infinite compression; the gods calm at once when they realize that nothing harms them when they stop radiating wrath, as there is no other wrath radiating back to them. That realization opens the way for the gods to find their own wisdom, to moderate their omnipotent authority habit, and to enjoy being one with all creatures instead of absolutely alienated from them. The gods become grateful disciples and colleagues of the adept, supporters of the enlightenment movement's redesign of the cosmos as a vessel of enlightenment rather than a theater of endless conflict—and, of course, the gods, so transformed, are all of us.

In the sacred history of the transformation of the wild frontier land of Tibet, we find a blueprint for completing the taming of our own wild world, where we keep building up the walls of enlightenment institutions and the local deities of collectivism, militarism, utilitarianism, stinginess, and fanaticism keep tearing them down. We need our own Padma Sambhava and Shantarakshita.

Perhaps in our case we will go through a different process. Perhaps we each must be our own emperor. We do not have the institution of kingship. In modern democracy, each of us is the king inasmuch as we vote for our rulers. We can see to it that the government does what we want. We must, each of us, invite our abbot-teachers and engage in a process of learning. We must, each of us, invite our adept-guide and engage in a poetic journey, a vision quest for the creation of the mandala of an enlightened America.

To finish building the free society dreamed of by Washington, Franklin, and Jefferson, we must draw upon the resources of the enlightened imagination, which can be systematically developed by the spiritual sciences of India and Tibet. We have not yet tamed our own demons of racism, nationalism, sexism, and materialism. We have not yet made peace with a land we took by force and have only partly paid for. We are a teeming conglomeration of people from different tribes who have yet to embrace fully the humanness in one another. And none of us can be really free until all of us are.

Chapter 8

INNER MODERNITY

*H*idden in the last thousand years of Tibet's civilization is a continuous process of inner revolution and cool evolution. In spiritual history, Tibet has been the secret dynamo that throughout this millennium has slowly turned the outer world toward enlightenment. Thus Tibetan civilization's unique role on the inner plane of history assumes a far greater importance than material history would indicate.

During the centuries following Padma Sambhava's taming of the nation, his adept disciples continued their mission on the grass-roots level, transforming local customs and moving the hearts of individuals from egocentric obsession to enlightened awareness. As a result of this persistent effort, monasteries and schools were built and local Tibetan nobles and regional kings began to send small missions to India to find more teachings, to invite important masters, and to restore the momentum of the development of civilization.

India was a vast place with a climate hard for Tibetans, and there were hostile kingdoms on the way. In 1040, the king of western Tibet sent a group to India to invite one of the greatest adepts of the day, the universally acclaimed spiritual master Atisha. When Atisha received the invitation, he consulted his oracle, the goddess Tara, who told him that his going to Tibet would be more helpful to the world than his staying in India, though his personal life span would be foreshortened by seventeen years. Atisha traveled to Tibet, stayed there for twelve years until his death, and sparked a great resurgence of the enlightenment movement.

Atisha's famous dictum was "All teachings are free of contradictions, since all have impact as practical instructions. In this way you easily discover the intent of the Buddha and guard against schisms between the teachings." His teaching essentially restored a sense of immediacy to the enlightenment practices and promoted the notion that it is possible for anyone to achieve enlightenment. At the same time, Atisha countered the idea that enlightenment could be achieved with no discipline at all.

When Atisha arrived in Tibet, monastic practitioners were limiting themselves to strict moral and ritual observances, and they considered messianic and apocalyptic teachings too advanced and dangerous. The apocalyptic practitioners considered the monastics too backward and thought themselves too developed to worry any longer about their own moral states. Atisha taught his thousands of disciples

how to integrate the monastic, messianic, and apocalyptic vehicles of practice into a single, comprehensive methodology.

The key to this integration of the three vehicles was the
practitioner's relationship with the lama, or spiritual teacher.
Atisha included the entire path, from the initial turning to
the Dharma up to the attainment of the highest enlightenment, within the context of the lama-disciple relationship.
Through the lama, each generation anew could experience
the immediate presence of Shakyamuni Buddha, since the
teachings were passed in an unbroken lineage from Shakyamuni Buddha to the lama, and everything that any disciple
knows of Buddha's teachings, which are based on the Buddha's own personal experience, comes from the lama. By
cultivating a relationship with a spiritual master, the practitioner opens the possibility of rapid realization.

The lama figure became a kind of magnifying glass that intensified the solar rays of teaching to kindle the minds of
the practitioners. The lama's actions carried an emphasis on
ethics, education, and monastic or yogic discipline, and thus
the danger of authoritarian abuse of this powerful role was
controlled. In the advanced stages of the path, the lama role
was integrated into the process of initiation into the tantric
mandala, during which the lama was visualized as insepara-
ble from all buddhas.

Tibetan seekers found this method of practice to be so ef-
ficacious that thousands of them began to attain the transformative stages of enlightenment. It is said that the hillsides

and retreats of central Tibet were ablaze with the light generated by profound concentrations, penetrating insights, and magnificent deeds of enthusiastic practitioners. The entire populace was moved by the energy released by individuals breaking through their age-old ignorance and prejudices and realizing enlightenment. Monastic universities were built in many localities and became the centers of community life— the schools, temples, hospitals, theaters, and also the centers of reason and therefore of order and authority.

Four more centuries of transforming the nation into a monastic university followed, wherein each individual's war with his or her own demons could be fought and won. On the local level, it was the beginning of the unique Tibetan monasticized society, in which the monastic community no longer represented the cool-revolutionary counterculture to which individuals on the freedom quest could repair to avoid routine duties. It gradually moved into the cool-evolutionary role of turning the counterculture into the mainstream transmitter of national values.

At a midpoint in this evolution, in southern Tibet in the early twelfth century, the yogin Milarepa became the first ordinary Tibetan to experience perfect enlightenment—buddhahood attained in a single short lifetime through the practice of tantric inner high technology. The life of Milarepa is one of the great classics of Tibetan literature as well as a world classic of spiritual autobiography. Milarepa was a commoner, the son of a prosperous peasant trader. His father died while Milarepa was an infant, and the boy and his mother and sister fell on hard times under an oppressive uncle who took control of the inheritance. Milarepa grew up determined to have revenge—as an adult, he apprenticed to a black magician and killed off all his uncle's descendants. He eventually repented and, after a long search for a teacher, became the disciple of the great translator and spiritual master Marpa. Marpa put Mila through Herculean ordeals to redirect the negative evolutionary impetus he had generated by killing so many people. Although Milarepa begged and pleaded, Marpa would not agree to teach him until Mila was on the point of suicide. Finally, Milarepa was initiated into the highest tantric teachings. He spent twenty years in meditation retreats in high mountain caves, emerging when he became completely enlightened.

Milarepa is especially beloved by Tibetans because he gave teachings to the common people, imbedding the highest doctrines in the familiar patterns of folk songs and ballads, making the practices accessible to all levels of society. Though he himself was not a monk nor trained in a monastic university, Milarepa entrusted his thousands of followers to a close disciple, the monk Gampopa, who organized the movement into a monastic university-based order in keeping with the needs of society at the time.

Because of their backgrounds, Marpa and Milarepa also were instrumental in breaking the lock the Tibetan aristocrats had on the power in the country. Their new order had no alignment with a noble family, as both Marpa and Milarepa had been commoners. There was no bloodline to transmit, as both lacked blood heirs. After several generations, the teachers chosen to lead this order were seen as the reincarnations of the teacher of the previous generation. This institution of reincarnation became of great importance in the Tibetan development of a cool-fruitional society and ultimately became the method for choosing the leader of the country. Leadership charisma and social authority were thereby divorced from the bloodlines of aristocratic families. It became widely accepted that a commoner could become a great spiritual master—a successful psychonaut or great adept, capable of manifesting his rebirth in conditions of his or her own choosing. Thus, a number of important adept-teachers, a few years after death, would reappear in the bodies of young children and demand to be returned to their previous monastic universities. After demonstrating perfect memory of secrets known only to their closest attendants, such adepts were formally accepted as reincarnations of the master and invested with the full authority of their previous lives. They were also provided with a strict and highly focused education to restore their full knowledge and powers of previous lives. To no one's surprise, these reincarnations were often child prodigies, able to read and write without learning, memorize hundreds of pages effortlessly, gain insight with ease, and give illuminating elucidations of difficult points after quick study of a subject.

Whatever the spiritual reality of these reincarnations, the social impact of this form of leadership was immense. It sealed the emerging spirituality of Tibetan society, in that death, which ordinarily interrupts progress in any society, could no longer block positive development. Just as Shakyamuni could be present to the practitioner through the initiation procedure and the sophisticated visualization techniques, so fully realized saints and sages were not withdrawn by death from their disciples, who depended on them to attain fulfillment. They kept coming back again and again as long as they were needed. They also no longer conceded social power to the militaristic aristocracy but insisted on the primacy of enlightenment in all realms of life.

The whole social development was extraordinary—with individual self-transformative practice centered in the monastic institutions; with the preservation of the ancient rites and contemplations that kept the nativistic energies tame and harnessed to the good; with the cultivation of scholarship and artistry; with the administration of the political system by enlightened hierarchs; with ascetic charisma diffused among the common people; and with the development of the reincarnation institution. It was a process of the removal of deep roots in instinct and cultural patterns. It was constantly threatened by inner resistance and by pressure from powerful neighbors beyond Tibet. For the most part, they were able to turn some of those neighbors, particularly the Mongolians, into friends.

During the thirteenth century, the great spiritual and diplomatic skill of the enlightened scholar-statesmen Sakya Pandita and his nephew Pakpa kept the Mongol conquerors from overrunning Tibet. The great emperor Qubilai, whom Marco Polo admired so much, chose Pakpa as his personal preceptor, and later Mongol emperors became more and more devoted to Tibetan Buddhism. In the fourteenth century, great works of self-transformation, inner science, artistic creativity, and international diplomacy were conducted by a number of outstanding geniuses in the various religious orders such as the scholar Buton Rinpoche (1310–1368) and the mystic philosopher Longchen Rabjamba (1308–1363). Their achievements and the evolution of the Tibetan people prepared the ground for the pivotal inner transformation that occurred around 1400, ushering in the Tibetan renaissance, strikingly synchronous with the European Renaissance of Petrarch (1304–1374) and da Vinci (1452–1519). This renaissance was triggered by the inner events associated with the enlightenment of Tibet's greatest spiritual and intellectual genius, Tsong Khapa (1357–1419).

Tsong Khapa was a spiritual prodigy. He studied with many masters in various monastic universities and withdrew from society time and again for intensive contemplation on the teachings he received. He had numerous visionary encounters with the buddhas thought to have existed throughout the ages, especially Manjushri, the bodhisattva of transcendent wisdom. In 1398, after years of arduous spiritual exercises and penetrating contemplations at a high mountain retreat, Tsong Khapa attained complete enlightenment. His world turned inside out, just the opposite of what he had expected. He perceived a cosmic shift from universe to buddhaverse, he met Shakyamuni Buddha face-to-face, and he realized that the world had been pure all along.

Up until the time of Tsong Khapa, ordinary Tibetans, with notable exceptions, tended to a primarily religious understanding of the Buddha's enlightenment. That is to say, they had faith in the Buddha and the bodhisattvas; they believed the teachings were good and should be followed. They considered their time a dark age, far from the fruitional time of Buddha himself. They considered India the Holy Land, and Tibet a land of human problems. Many people had a sense that the Dharma was in its last days, and beyond praying and having faith, there was little a human being could do. Enlightenment as a personal possibility was thought of as remote, an ideal attainable by only the few.

After mastering all the branches of the teaching, Tsong Khapa implemented them in newly lucid and vital formulations, creating a curriculum that could be followed by anyone. Enlightenment became more than a possibility—it became widely accessible, with tens of thousands of persons freeing themselves of their fetters and confusions. This tremendous release of energy caused by thousands of minds becoming totally liberated in a short time was a planetary phenomenon, like a great spiritual pulsar emitting enlightenment in waves broadcast around the globe.

Tsong Khapa set forth during the last twenty-one years of

his life to transform Tibet from an ordinary society attuned to an ordinary universe into an unprecedented, extraordinary society attuned to the buddhaversal reality. He traveled from place to place teaching multitudes of ardent seekers and created a congress to renew the monastic discipline, the foundational evolutionary regime of the inner revolution.

In 1939, Tsong Khapa organized a festival celebrating the coming of the future Buddha, Maitreya, and, in 1409, a national yearly festival of enlightenment. During each New Year, this festival dissolved the barrier between the sacred land of Buddha and the routine land of Tibet, and all ordinary activity was suspended for a mass celebration of the immanence of enlightenment. The Tibetan people as a whole, not just the adepts, perceived visions of buddhas and deities in the sky above, day after day, over entire regions and provinces. The people no longer thought of Shakyamuni and others as lost in history but felt the immediate presence of enlightened beings, their radiant love and boundless generosity, and the availability of their skillful arts of liberation to anyone who resolved to perceive them here and now.

Everything became possible for any individual, no longer born too late or too early, no longer having to put personal desire for evolution on hold for mundane duties. Thus Tibet became a land where the horizon for individual development was as infinite as anyone could desire.

The Great Prayer Festival continued from then on with few interruptions until the twentieth century. It is a festival

like Rosh Hashanah for Jews or Easter for Christians, a festival that commemorates a moment of eternity, a moment
when all wishes are fulfilled, when the power of compassion
is manifest, the immediacy of grace is experienced. It is a
time for millennial or apocalyptic consciousness, a time of
the end of time, a time beyond progression.

What is this millennial consciousness or apocalyptic
awareness? How does it differ from our ordinary consciousness? As we know, our ordinary consciousness is distorted by
the mistake of thinking ourselves to be the absolute center
in a world of many absolute entities, a world in which we experience great suffering when these others impinge on us in
our position at the center of the universe. When we begin to
see the tensions inherent in this predicament, we visualize a
state of release from the prison of thinking "It's me, it's me,
I'm it, I'm the one." We may hope for this release, or even
work toward it, but basic to our present state of consciousness is our deep feeling that it is impossible to actually experience such release in this lifetime.

Millennial or apocalyptic consciousness, on the other
hand, develops when a person breaks through the shell of habitual self-centeredness, sees through the falsely created view
of the absoluteness of the ordinary world, and realizes truth
in an instant. A healthy person in the melting aspect of the
moment of full orgasm loses himself or herself completely
and has an instance of apocalypse before the structures and
boundaries of inadequacy return with all their force. People

absorbed in activity—runners racing, musicians performing, artists creating, mothers giving milk—all of them have
a taste of millennial consciousness, a momentary blissful
freedom from dissatisfaction, self-concern, and pain. This
consciousness in the enlightenment movement is called millennial when the vision of this freedom expands so greatly
that it aims to create a nationwide and ultimately a worldwide society of perfect happiness based on enlightenment. It
is apocalyptic in the sense of being instantaneously revelatory
and ultimately decisive.

In Tibet, the monastic universities became factories for
the development of enlightened people who could experience this consciousness continuously. Building on the Great
Prayer Festival energy of Tsong Khapa, a new wave of intensive monasticization swept the fifteenth and sixteenth
centuries. Many people were inspired to embark on the voy-
age of the discovery of the reality of their souls, to find the
fountain of immortal wisdom, and they needed institutions
to support their adventures. Tibetans had no great wealth,
but they had sufficient materials for keeping the body comfortable enough to work on spiritual development. The only
way to develop true freedom was to cultivate the soul
through education, purification, and realization.

There ensued a vast expansion of monastic universities.
Between two and three thousand new monastic cities were
built anew over the next centuries, and another two or three
thousand old centers were renovated and expanded.

Though exact figures are hard to come by, approximately one-sixth of the roughly eight million Tibetans of those days entered the huge monastic cities that were springing up all over the country. By the late sixteenth century, perhaps more than a million people were intellectually developed through this education process, and perhaps several hundreds of thousands had opened powerful new enlightenment energies in their minds.

The wave of liberated energy began to spread to the Mongols, Turks, Manchurians, Chinese, and other Himalayan peoples. The economy and politics of Tibet slowly shifted to reflect this movement, and the seed of the final form of Tibetan society was planted. By the seventeenth century, the apocalyptic countercultures of the monastics and adepts were fully fused with the mainstream and became the actual culture of the society.

At this very time, an enlightenment was taking place outside Asia as well. The Western Renaissance can be described as the reemergence of self-confidence in the human's ability to understand the universe and as the movement away from the notion of God as absolute authoritarian patriarch to God as divine reason, enlightened understanding, and compassion and love in action. It was a new perception of human genius as being in line with the nature of the universe, stimulated by the rediscovery of the humanism of the ancient Greeks. This Renaissance self-confidence liberated energy for personal evolution in daily life, making possible the progressive development of science and great achievements in the arts.

People began to expand their horizons intellectually and spiritually, and the development of the European oceanic empires accelerated the globalization process that had been under way since the Buddha's time.

The tragedy for the Europeans was that the partial success achieved in the development of human consciousness from the Renaissance to the Enlightenment was followed by a short-circuiting of the Christian monastic institution, a shutting down of its own inner-revolution approach. Although on one level this shutdown was compensated for by the development of the secular university model, on another it left the social space open for militarism to dominate. Society focused its new self-confidence on materialistic mastery of the physical world. When people felt their energy flow into channels seeking immediate inner satisfaction, they became afraid. So they diverted the millennial power of confidence and activism outwardly into progressive materialism, industrial productivity, and militarism. The very existence of the spirit was eventually denied, and matter became the sole constant within a nihilistic cosmos.

Millennial consciousness is the felt sense of the all-positive in immediate presence and effective action. In Tibet, the Great Prayer Festival guaranteed the best of possibilities for everyone. People's feelings of being in an apocalyptic time in a specially blessed and chosen land—in their own form of a

"New Jerusalem," a Kingdom of Heaven manifest on earth—
had a powerful effect on the whole society. The goal was not
to live for today by getting the most out of the material moment. Rather, it was to move toward total access to the most
effective methods of individual evolutionary development
that would lead to a total and permanent liberation in an
eternity of blissful moments. There was a sense of support
from each individual in the whole community to bend every
effort toward the final positive, even if one could not get that
far oneself, knowing that many others were fully engaged on
that path.

The apocalyptic world picture allows for a very high level
of individual self-confidence and energy fulfillment. Millennial consciousness, the consciousness of living in a sacred
realm, thus entered the fruitional phase in Tibet, allowing
every person to manifest full energy in the present moment
and life, moving each one toward personal development and
fulfillment.

There are striking parallels among, and at the same time a
strange inversion of the developments in, Tibet and those in
the West and the rest of Asia as they began their different
processes of modernization from the sixteenth century on,
the takeoff point for the industrial revolution and the rise of
secular modernity. The great social scientist Max Weber bril-
liantly traced the industrial work ethic to the selfless, cor-

porate, economic discipline of the European monastery. Paradoxically, its asceticism—or nonconsumption—brought great wealth accumulation. Looking at the evolution of this monastic asceticism into the industrial capitalist work ethic, Weber discovered its source in the Protestant transformation of the medieval universe, wherein sacred and secular had been kept in balance.

The pre-Copernican cosmos presented the flat earth as the center of God's attention, a kind of staging area on which human beings lived to see whether they would qualify for eternal heaven or hell. The ideal was life as a monastic in service of and prayer to God; the worldly arena was considered a playground for sinners and a testing ground for potentially salvageable souls.

Thought was strictly controlled by the Church's inquisition, and social life was dominated by the Church through its network of cathedrals and monasteries, its calendar of festivals, and its all-pervading ideology. But political life was ruled by warring nobles—their lust for power went unchecked except by the limits of technology and the need to retain some legitimacy in the eyes of the Church. Rome had been trying to tame the European warlords for centuries but was hampered by operating on only one side of the sacred/secular duality. The Christian monastic inner revolution, just like the Buddhist in most Asian countries, remained strictly countercultural. At times, its monastic army was coopted and even used militarily in crusades.

In the fifteenth century, European energies began to boil over. New scientific discoveries emerged: the Copernican shift from a God-dominated, anthropocentric world to a vaster, less neat universe with man more on his own; the Columbian shift from flat earth to a round one with uncharted lands and vast exploitable resources; and the Galilean shift from a world of mathematical design, strict teleology, and immutable laws prescribed by Aristotle to a world of far greater complexity and aimless mechanism, ready for empirical investigation.

The Protestant Reformation in the sixteenth century began the process of secularization of the sacred in the West, in which a materialistic nonduality was achieved by the absorption of the sacred into the secular. Tremendous intellectual and productive energies were released and directed toward the conquest of nature, the technological conquest of physical forces, and the political and economic conquest of the planet.

Encouraged by the new rationalism and by the corruption of monastic and religious institutions, Luther, Zwingli, and Calvin broke away from the Catholic Church and placed salvation more squarely in the hands of God, leaving people little to do in saving themselves. Meanwhile, life on earth might as well be fruitful and productive.

The essence of the process of secularization was that traditionally sacred limitations of human thought and action were removed. Reason was no longer a divine faculty built into people for the purpose of discovering the glory of God, but became an instrument merely for working the human will upon nature, gaining advantage and leverage over the mechanical processes of body and environment to exploit them for immediate benefit.

With no need to devote any energy toward salvation, one was able to devote all one's life energy to mundane activity, business, and production. The monastery, as a bastion of spiritual development, became superfluous to society. Monks and nuns were seen as perfectionists, vainly trying to alter their fates by self-purification and mortification. Thousands of monasteries in northern Europe were closed during this time, and the monastic work ethic of rational, selflessly impersonal, corporate production was unleashed into the secular realm to become the basis of capitalism and industrial production. The universities became central to the process of education, and new professions emerged to provide services that had been performed by monks and nuns—law, medicine, and education, to name a few.

The economies of Europe began to expand tremendously, generating great military might and unprecedented secular development. The industrial revolution was on, fueled by the Protestant ethic and its secularizing ideology, scientific innovations, voyages of resource discovery and wealth exploitation, and the appetite for world conquest. The closing of the monasteries made more people available to go to war.

In the new order, the spiritual and material realms became radically disjointed. The spiritual world was estranged from the material and ultimately became "other" to the world of material things. As a result, humans believed they had no leverage over their spiritual destinies. Luther's "salvation through faith alone" initiated the trend; Calvin's predestination removed all human control; Descartes reduced mind and spirit to a sizeless point of absolute subjectivity; and Kant's transcendental ego removed the spiritual self from practical relevance. The actual person, along with God, got abstracted out of existence, subtracted from what matters. The corresponding northern European destruction of monasticism as a balancing force in society resulted in a "this-worldly asceticism," wherein the entire life energy is turned over to worldly activity, which is selfless in that it lacks ultimate fruition. It was natural that material progress became a new absolute, infinite in horizon, with the removal of the medieval notions of life in balance with nature and of nature as sacred in the sense of being God-created.

By the seventeenth century, these trends had developed a full head of steam. The cosmos was seen as a mechanism, perhaps started by a divine artificer and scientist but now running on automatic. The planet was there to be enjoyed by the human mechanisms that inhabited this larger machine. The monastery and cathedral were replaced by the university. The entire universe was disenchanted.

In the northern Protestant states and in England after Cromwell executed Charles I in 1649, the divine right of kings began to look less and less plausible. The utilitarian modern mind began to assert control over every aspect of social and political life, beginning a process that culminated in the American and French revolutions of the late eighteenth century. The great ocean empires of the Atlantic powers, first Portugal, Spain, Holland, and eventually England and France, began the process of globalization we have inherited today.

Many have sought to explain how Europe came to dominate the planet. The changes that created modernity were not mere technological innovations, not the mere accidental discovery of the New World, with its vast riches and resources, but the Europeans' new sense that the world was their oyster, that they lived in a world where God no longer cared to restrain their every impulse. Society could be reorganized in whatever way was most efficient. Agriculture could be reorganized for maximum yield, and industry could produce maximum profit. The very elements of nature could be recombined in powerful chemistries to create nearly any effect. Machines could enhance human efforts and perceptions to a previously unimaginable degree. There were no limits, no guarantees, no rewards without adventure, and probably no punishment for the successful.

No Western writer has yet thought to attribute the European drive to world exploration and domination to Europe's underdevelopment, poverty, and relatively barbaric and violent cultures. The compass and gunpowder—created in China but not used in conquest or violence—were immediately implemented by the more backward Europeans to dominate the Arab and Ottoman Muslims, then the peoples of the New World and Africa, and finally the highly civilized peoples of Asia. From the postmodern perspective, the so-called "rise" of the West looks completely different. No civilization prior to ours ever developed nuclear weapons and thus put itself in greater danger of its own total obliteration. Is bringing the human race and all life on earth to the brink of obliteration a sign of being advanced?

Painful as it may be to face, the obvious fact is that Europeans had to conquer Asia because they wanted what Asians naturally had—Columbus was looking for the passage to India, after all. The vast wealth of the Americas and Africa was insufficient for Europe's appetites. Europeans needed ever more powerful technologies because they felt weak and insecure. Their long experience of poverty, scarcity, and deprivation only whetted their appetite for limitless productivity.

This idea that Asia's failure to conquer Europe can be seen as a sign of its being more, not less, advanced than Europe is shattering to our materialist and militarist preconceptions. But if we go deeper, we can find a valuable consolation. For us to understand the nature of Tibet's inner modernity, we must analyze the five main transformations that Europe went through from Reformation to Enlightenment: (1) the unification of the life-world by the process of removing the sacred as relevant to human purpose, leaving an all-absorbing secular realm; (2) the disenchantment of the natural world, removing traditional concerns that had restrained its exploitation; (3) the rationalization of all human effort in the goal of maximizing human comfort during the temporary existence in the secular realm; (4) the absolutization of material progress; and (5) the destruction of the channel of effort toward the sacred (represented by monasticism and its organized striving for perfection), which had been the institutional brake against materialism, industrialism, and militarism, leaving all human enterprise focused on those three pursuits.

Each of these strands in the Western process of outer modernization corresponds, in the reverse, to a strand in the process undergone by Tibet in its inner modernization: (1) Instead of the life-world being unified by secularization, Tibet unified it by what we can call "sacralization"—the sacred gradually absorbing the secular. The ultimate perfection of the individual, the society, and even the buddhaverse became the prime concern of the whole society. The modernist unity of the sacred/secular dichotomy was achieved at the sacred, not the secular, pole; (2) instead of disenchantment, the whole of reality became reenchanted. The magical/ordinary dichotomy was resolved by all becoming magical, opposite from all becoming routine and mechanical. Since the inner science of the Buddhist curriculum is based on a sense of the mind's natural power over nature, the transformation of the mind became the main avenue of progress toward the transformation of nature; (3) actions and goals were totally rationalized in Tibet as in the West, but in Tibet the rational made everything in life instrumental for the individual's attainment of evolutionary perfection in buddhahood, perfect wisdom and complete compassion; (4) spiritual progress was the goal of absolute concern—the development of human perfection was industrialized—turning the whole of society into one vast school for enlightenment; and finally (5) while commercial materialism was always a part of the seminomadic Tibetan economy and lifestyle, monasticism became completely dominant over all other institutions, disarming the military, transmuting the warrior spirit of Tibetan militarism into the ascetical heroism of monastic and contemplative adepts.

Transformed, modern Tibet differed from traditional, medieval Tibet by its unification of the dualistic life-world in a thoroughgoing sacralization of worldview, culture, ethic, and economy, just as modern Europe differed from premodern, traditional Europe by its unification of the dualistic life-world through total secularization. So we must qualify what we have come to call "modernity" in the West as "materialistic" or "outer" modernity, and contrast it with a parallel but alternative Tibetan modernity qualified as "spiritualistic" or "inner" modernity.

While Europe was engaging in its outer conquest, Tibet was entering another phase of its inner conquest, following its enlightenment-movement renaissance. The millennial consciousness that Tsong Khapa tapped into at the beginning of the fifteenth century deepened over the next two hundred years, preparing the way for this next phase of Tibet's inner modernization. As Europe was pushing away the Pope, the Church, and the enchantment of everyday life, Tibet was turning over the reins of its country to a new kind of government, which cannot properly be called "theocratic," since Tibetans do not believe in an omnipotent God, but which can be called "buddhocratic."

Our common-era year of 1642 corresponds to the Tibetan Year of the Male Water Horse. In the great fortress of Gyantse, high over the plains of south central Tibet, the monk Losang Gyatso, His Holiness the Fifth Dalai Lama, a gentle genius, scholar, and reincarnate saint, was offered the throne to rule the one million square miles and six or seven million rather religious but earthy and diverse people of Tibet. The Qoshot Mongol warlord Gushri Khan gathered the Tibetan nobility, allies, and former enemies and led them to make this great offering. It put an end to a century of regional conflict imperfectly restrained by various religious orders whose own intellectual and religious rivalries often had been exploited by the political factions.

The entire nation had enjoyed the fervor of the millennialist expansion of monasticism that began at the end of the fourteenth century. But gradually, as more and more monasteries absorbed the resources, allegiance, and delight of the people, the nobility began to perceive the monastic movement as a threat to their social control. Aristocracy is based on the military order, and militarism cannot survive universal monasticization, just as monasticism cannot survive universal militarization. So the regional lords made a fierce effort to turn back the clock to a medieval dualistic society, with monastic holiness and militaristic governance in alternating balance. Their resistance to the millennialist tide led to the sixteenth century's agonizing social upheavals.

The most intense period of conflict nearly coincided with the Thirty Years War in Europe from 1618 to 1648, when the Holy Roman Empire attempted to reverse by force the Protestant decentralization of the Church. In Tibet, the disorder was so great that the Fifth Dalai Lama was raised from childhood in secrecy and the yearly Great Prayer Festival was suspended. The religious orders were drawn into the factionalism by association with particular warlord patrons, but the real conflict was not about religious rivalry. It was the final showdown in Tibet between militarism and monasticism. This same conflict was settled in Japan in favor of the militarists, with Nobunaga's destruction of the monasteries on Mount Hiei in 1571. It was settled in favor of the militarists also in northern Europe at the Peace of Westphalia in 1648, consolidating the Reformation and disenfranchising monasticism in the northern countries, where the industrial revolution and the militaristic world-conquest campaign would soon take over totally.

The situation in Tibet was resolved with the Fifth Dalai Lama's Mongolian patron's intervention to break the coalition of Tibetan warlords. Since the Mongolians were performing a religious service and were not interested in settling down in Tibet, the keys of the kingdom were handed over to the Dalai Lama himself. For the first time in Buddhist history, a full-fledged monk was crowned both secular and spiritual king.

The Fifth Dalai Lama did not base his new peace on an ascendancy of his order over other religious orders, backed by his triumphant warlord. Rather, his insight was that the real conflict was between the emerging inner modernity and the medieval society dominated by rival warlords. So the Dalai Lama advanced the radical new idea that the spiritual, monastic institutions of all the religious orders must assume both the social and political responsibilities for avoiding such civil wars in the future. The leader of this new government, the symbolic incarnation of the most revered deity of the land—Avalokiteshvara, the messiah bodhisattva of compassion—was His Holiness the Dalai Lama, who received the spiritual approval of the entire population.

Small wonder. Suppose the people of a Catholic country were to share a perception of a particular spiritual figure as not merely a representative of God, as in the Pope being the vicar of Christ, but as an actual incarnation of the Savior—or, say, an incarnation of the Archangel Gabriel. In such a situation it would not be strange for the nation to reach a point where the divine would actually take responsibility for the government. In Tibet, this moment was the culmination of centuries of grass-roots millennial consciousness, the political ratification of the millennial direction that had been intensifying since the Great Prayer Festival tradition had begun in 1409. The sense of the presence of an enlightened being was widespread enough for the people to join together after the last conflict and entrust to him their land and their fate.

The Dalai Lama accepted this responsibility and stepped into the social arena to tame the feuding warlords of the whole area of Tibet, Mongolia, China, and Manchuria. As a Buddhist monk, Losang Gyatso was celibate, propertyless, homeless, concerned first and foremost with the attainment of freedom from suffering and ignorance for himself and all other living beings. Shakyamuni Buddha had founded the inner revolution by leaving the throne of a kingdom to take up his monastic quest of enlightenment. How was Losang Gyatso to do the opposite, to accept responsibility for a huge country with millions of people while remaining a monk with spiritual priorities? For Losang Gyatso to remain a monk and yet take responsibility for the actual governance of a country was unprecedented in Buddhist history. Nevertheless, he created a planetary first, a national monastic Buddhist government, unifying the life-world of Tibet and absorbing the secular into the sacred. Unlike Emperor Ashoka's earlier top-down revolution, this one was overwhelmingly supported by the citizenry, who were heartily in accord with the new leader's spiritual goals. This support provided Losang Gyatso with the broad foundation that Ashoka had lacked.

Once crowned, the Great Fifth, as he is called, moved systematically to consolidate the millennial society and to help it become a world of universal perfect enlightenment. He completely disarmed the feudal nobility and proceeded to disband all Tibetan armies. Since he did not need to move troops around in a demilitarized Tibet, he did not build a national road system—wheeled vehicles were ineffective in the mountainous terrain anyway. Trade goods could be moved best by yak, horse, and camel caravans. Because the national budget was not needed for building cart roads, it could be devoted primarily to health, welfare, education, and celebration.

Having been given the responsibility for the entire land from the whole populace, the Fifth Dalai Lama expropriated all the land-owning nobility's ancestral holdings and returned about a third of the land, in estates, to each family as salary for government service. He used another third of the land to endow the ubiquitous monastic schools, unleashing an even greater wave of monastery building, in which he was joined by members of the older orders. And he kept the last third of the land as endowment for the new government, called the Ganden Palace Triumph Government, associating it with the future Buddha Maitreya, the Buddhist symbol of millennial consciousness.

The Great Fifth built a monumental official seat of government in Lhasa, the Potala, on the Red Mountain overlooking the city, around the ancient residence of Songzen Gampo, Tibet's first Dharma emperor one thousand years before. The Potala became the center of the energies of the new capital and functioned at the same time as monastery, palace, and sacred mandala, symbolizing the Dalai Lama's fusion of the roles of selfless monk, king, and great adept. It was a lofty spiritual center that radiated the unifying millennial consciousness of the nation.

The Great Fifth also changed all Tibetans' lives, bringing the fruitional effect of the inner revolution into daily reality for everyone. He abolished militarism and the feudal servitude of peasants in their warlords' armies; he rationalized the medieval networks of mutual social obligations into economic relationships. In converting all these relationships from military to economic, the government of the Fifth Dalai Lama continued the modernization of Tibet, freeing the maximum number of individuals to pursue their own inner inclinations and spiritual destinies, their own enlightenment education in the monastic universities, provided they satisfied the most minimal economic obligations to society. Also, Tibetan peasants and nomads were not dispossessed of their lands and forced to live in industrial slums, as they were in Europe. The Chinese Communists' propaganda that Tibet maintained a medieval serf society, or a system of slavery such as in the antebellum South, is simply a fabrication created to justify the utter devastation brought upon Tibet by the Chinese invasion, occupation, communization, and finally colonization and genocide.

In the modern West, we feel we are free individuals because everything is reducible to cash—there is abstract quantifiability of our entire worth and obligation. Yet the "cashability" of everything means also that everything is utterly alienable—we can lose absolutely everything at any time. As an individual in modern Tibet before the Chinese invasion, you were free to pursue spiritual development, pilgrimage, trade, or leisure; you were as vulnerable as any living thing to the radical dispossession of death, but you had inalienable links to the productive earth you could count on for yourself and your family in this life.

While the Great Fifth was transforming Tibet, major transformations were happening elsewhere on the planet. In 1642, Galileo died and Isaac Newton was born (if not his reincarnation, certainly his intellectual successor). The Sun King, Louis XIV of France, was born in 1638, soon to begin his great unification of France around his newly built palace at Versailles, construction proceeding slightly in the wake of that of the Dalai Lama's Potala. In the 1640s, Oliver Cromwell led his Ironsides into battle against Charles I of England, beginning trends that led to parliamentary democracy, modern militarism, and secularism in government. In 1644, the Manchus had their first success in the conquest of China, replacing the Ming dynasty. In the 1630s, John Harvard was endowing Harvard University. In 1642, the Tokugawa shoguns consolidated their secular power over Japan. The haiku poet Basho was hard at work during the last part of the seventeenth century. In 1613, the Romanov dynasty was founded in Russia, soon spreading from Europe to Siberia, but Peter the Great didn't begin to build St. Petersburg intil 1703. The Dutch bought and began to settle Manhattan island in 1626. In 1642, Rembrandt painted *The Night Watch*, and Tasman discovered New Zealand. Queen Christina of Sweden took back her kingdom in 1660. Descartes was working on the ramifications of having made individual self-evidence the basis of valid knowledge. The Moghul dynasty in Delhi was developing the culture that produced the Taj Mahal. The Safavid dynasty was at its peak in Iran until 1629, and Shah Abbas inaugurated the magnificent Isfahan capital. The Ottomans built the Blue Mosque. The Holy Roman Empire of the Habsburgs, tired of the Thirty Years War, gave up its drive to reverse the Reformation and concluded the Peace of Westphalia with the northern princes in 1648.

The recent appearance of modern consciousness in the industrial world is not something radically new or unprecedented. Modern consciousness has been developed all over Asia in the Buddhist subcultures for thousands of years. From the enlightenment perspective, the human approaching liberation becomes more and more individuated, more and more open and free from any fixity, more and more rational and multidimensional in increasingly complex interrelation-ships. Once we concede the existence of such a structure of consciousness in other civilizations, we can assume that it was studied and analyzed before, and that methods of culti-vating it, improving it, and overcoming its aberrations and obstructions already have been expounded. Once we un-hitch modernity from its Western, materialistic form, we can think creatively of alternatives to our current fixations without conceding defeat and seeking to revert to premod-ern consciousness and lifestyles. Since we have discerned that nondualism, whether secularized or sacralized, is the essence of what's good about modernity, instead of retreat-ing from history and reverting to monistic, nonrational con-sciousness and its attendant social collectivism, we can move on to a creative nondualism.

This nondualism is experienced in the individual mind as unity of self and world, a sense of being ultimately a part of the world, involved in its every aspect, combined with a feel-ing of being of essential, unique importance to that world. When it is felt as an inner understanding, it gives a slight, de-licious shudder of release. It relieves one's ancient, ingrained notion of having been divided—of the body and senses en-gaged in an uncomfortable, confusing process of living; of an alienated self inexplicably outside of that process, incom-prehensibly controlled by an absolute power and authority. That alienated absolute, called God or Soul, has been a mind block in humans, built by ancient cultures on an instinctual shock mechanism of primordial inheritance—a kind of sen-

sibility cutoff valve useful in hard conditions of animal life—
in order to hobble human minds, enslave them from within
the core of their programs by making them feel no confidence in their own powers of knowing or being, which in
turn makes people amenable to manipulation by irrational
authorities and fixes them in ignorance of their real nature.

In 1400 and continuing in the seventeenth century, brave
individuals West and East broke that hobbling block, broke
through the confusions of dualism and subsequently developed new senses of relativity, responsibility, and conscious
individual autonomy. This breakthrough is what we have
been calling millennial or apocalyptic consciousness.

The Western outer modernity led the European nations
to militarize and arm industrially, conquer all traditional
nations and the entire material world, and eventually jeop-
ardize the whole planetary environment through their addiction to infinite productivity and infinite consumption.
The Tibetan inner modernity led Tibet to monasticize industrially and disarm unilaterally, abdicate the struggle for
physical expansion and conquest, and conquer all the inner
frontiers needed to achieve enlightenment, seen as the complete mastery of mind and body, time and space, and all the
processes of death, in-between states, and life.

The challenge before us now is how to integrate outer and
inner modernities to create a balanced, healthy, comfortable, enlightenment-oriented lifestyle that will be viable with
wide variation on a global scale for the twenty-first century.

Chapter 9

HOPE FOR
THE THIRD
MILLENNIUM

The Reunion of Outer and Inner

*T*ibet's inward turn led to its neglect of outer realities and resulted in its isolation from the rest of the world. Inner modernity would soon be overrun by the violent tendencies of the twentieth century's outer modernity.

One of the few creative forces countering this wild destructiveness was Mahatma Gandhi, who synthesized the teachings of Buddha, Jesus, Thoreau, and Tolstoy into a political method of nonviolent activism. A visionary clearly too far ahead of this century of violence, he did succeed in finally getting the British to withdraw from their most prized colonial possession, but then he was assassinated and could not prevent Indian independence from leading to the violent schism between Hindu and Muslim.

Gandhi argued that there are three responses to evil. The lowest and least recommended response is to submit to evil, to surrender and do its bidding in abject docility. The second response is to fight evil with evil, to oppose it violently. The best response to evil is nonviolent resistance, to fight against evil without adopting evil tactics. It takes the greatest courage of all, combined with unwavering intelligence and compassion, to stand up against evil without fighting it violently. For people to resist the Nazis, they would have had to have stood en masse in the streets in front of the tanks and firing squads, letting themselves be killed rather than obeying any order. Gandhi's experiences in South Africa and India had taught him that this action would eventually force the German soldiers to come to terms with the fact that they were not fighting an enemy but were committing atrocities against all reason and all nature. Their evil command structure would then crumble, and the war would end. Gandhi admitted that this high road of nonviolence would result in many casualties before the killers relented, but he pointed out that violent resistance also would cause high numbers of casualties; in fact, it destroyed the whole of Europe and the flower of entire generations.

After about two hundred years of millennial civilization progressing in the direction set by the Great Fifth Dalai Lama, Tibet's inner peace and sovereign stability began to be eroded by imperial pressures from beyond its borders. The Manchus, who by the nineteenth century had lost much of their original appreciation of Tibet's role of spiritual peacemaker, became more and more aggressive toward Tibet, carved off about one-third of its territory in the northeast, and became more intrusive in the capital at Lhasa. The fact that no Dalai Lama lived beyond thirty years of age all through the nineteenth century indicates the Manchu manipulation of various regents to insure that no leader strong enough to make independent decisions would arise.

Such was the political reality when Tubten Gyatso (1876–1934), the Great Thirteenth Dalai Lama, was discovered in 1878. Just before completing his classical Buddhist education and assuming the responsibility of ruling the country in the 1890s, he discovered a plot against his life and defeated it. Once in office, he reviewed the international situation and saw the Tibetan and Mongolian monastic nations surrounded by the British Indian, Ottoman, Russian, and Manchu empires. Since the nation lacked any defense force and had to be defended by diplomacy, he chose to ally with the major power farthest away and least likely to interfere in Tibet's affairs, which was Russia.

The British reacted with fear to this nominal connection and in 1904 invaded Tibet for the purpose of making a treaty of alliance and protection with the Dalai Lama. Misunderstanding Britain's intentions, the Dalai Lama fled to Mongolia and Beijing. Finally realizing that the Manchus themselves were a greater threat to Tibet than the British, he returned to Tibet. When the Chinese pursued him there, he fled for his life right on through Tibet and down to Darjeeling, into the arms of the British in India.

The Manchu empire collapsed in 1911, and the Thirteenth Dalai Lama was able to return to Tibet. He was received with great joy by the Tibetan people, and the small Manchu garrisons still left in Tibet were rounded up unharmed, marched down to Darjeeling, and deported back to China through Calcutta. And with that the Great Thirteenth Dalai Lama began the process of trying to fit inner modernity together with outer modernity, amid the violent disruptions caused by imperialism and genocidal ideologies in the chaotically developing twentieth century.

The Great Thirteenth understood that none of the European powers would do much to help Tibet. No Chinese emperor ever had successfully invaded Tibet because of the high altitudes and tremendous distances involved. But now regional warlords from China's western provinces were armed with modern weapons and inclined to a new kind of adventure. Tibet had to establish itself in the twentieth-century nation-state system. Imperial modernity was coming to an end. Democratic modernity was just beginning. Now it was every nation for itself. So he began to create a secular education system modeled on the British, a new mint, an armory, a defense force, a postal service, a national flag, and a more sophisticated foreign ministry. He went into a three-year retreat, from 1914 to 1917, to adjust his own psyche to this new reality. He emerged from the retreat with great energy and began to tackle the various groups of traditionalists within Tibet. The aristocrats did not want to pay the higher taxes required to maintain a defense force. The monastics did not want a widespread secular education system, nor did they want to pay taxes from their lands for the army.

Frustrated in large measure by the intrigues of the world powers, by the isolationism of his own people, and by the savage Russian Communist treatment of Outer Mongolia in 1932, the Great Thirteenth consciously decided to pass through the reincarnation process a decade early, in order to be old enough to be of some help during the terrible times coming to Tibet that he foresaw.

The Great Thirteenth left a number of clues to the where-abouts of his reincarnation. Investigations over the next few years turned up signs pointing to the northeast and to a white house with turquoise-blue tiles on the roof. A search party went out, and after a long journey the party finally reached a house matching the description, in the province of Amdo. The members of the party had a strong intuition about the place, so they disguised themselves by wearing one another's clothes—the Great Thirteenth's chamberlain wore those of the groom, the groom wore monk's robes, and so forth. A beautiful child named Lhamo Dondrub came into the kitchen, went up to the chamberlain, who was dressed as the groom, and, when asked, identified him as the "lama from Sera." The boy recognized all the objects of the Great Thirteenth, turning away from the prettier, newer alternatives. The boy then announced to his family that he was going with the men to Lhasa. All the members of the party were sure he was the right child, but they pretended not to be, since they had to persuade the local warlord to let the boy go with them. So they chose several additional candidates as a cover and escorted the young lamas to Kumbum monastery and eventually to Lhasa.

The new Fourteenth Dalai Lama, born in 1935, grew up much as had his predecessors, spending the bulk of his time in studies, memorizing long texts of prayer, ritual, philosophy, psychology, and ethics. Once he knew the classics by heart, he began to study the vast commentarial literature. He also began debating with partners about the meanings of what he was reading and studying, debating being the essential method for sharpening the ability to think critically and thereby for reaching deeper understanding in contemplation. Finally he would come to a point in a particular subject when it would be necessary for him to take a short contemplative retreat, to deeply imprint upon himself and embody whatever he had understood.

The Dalai Lama's curriculum included also the history of Tibet and the biographies of his predecessors. He chose on his own to pursue some foreign studies, reading books on world culture and history. He was particularly fascinated with tools and gadgets: movie projectors, cameras, watches, automobiles, even guns. He learned something of Western technology and ways of thinking from the German expatriate mountain climber Heinrich Harrer.

When the Dalai Lama was still only fourteen, the Chinese Communists defeated the Nationalists and took over China proper. Within the year, Chinese armies entered eastern Tibet, and the following year, 1950, they launched a full-scale invasion of central Tibet. The Tibetans formally enthroned the Dalai Lama as ruler of the country, five years early, and then the entire government fled to the Indian border. After realizing that the outer world would do little to help, they decided to return to Lhasa to try to work with the Chinese Communists. A year or two later, the Dalai Lama traveled to Beijing for several months to visit with Mao and discuss Tibet's future. The idealistic young lama had a momentary feeling that perhaps China might help him develop the outer modern aspect of his country, though Mao's chilling whisper, "Religion is poison," at the end of their meeting gave him serious misgivings.

Once he returned to Tibet, he began to experience the reality of the invasion as the Chinese generals in charge of Tibet broke promise after promise. The Chinese created food shortages, expropriated lands and goods, began to brainwash common Tibetans, and violently persecuted the majority, who would not agree to their ideas.

By 1956 it became clear to the Dalai Lama that he could not effectively help his people under the constraints imposed by the Chinese occupation army in Tibet. Then, in 1959, the Chinese generals in Tibet tried to seize the Dalai Lama, either to kill him or to keep him under their control as a hostage. Under the cover of a freak dust storm, he escaped through the Chinese lines surrounding Lhasa and, after an arduous journey fleeing military pursuit, finally reached asylum in India.

In the wake of his departure, the Chinese slaughtered hundreds of thousands of Tibetans. Tibetan culture was systematically assaulted—people were arrested, tortured, and killed for possessing an image of the Buddha or the Dalai Lama or for bowing to a sacred monument. Schools were destroyed, books burned, and the Tibetan language suppressed. Monasteries were razed, the monks and nuns killed, imprisoned, or forced to break their vows in public. Tibet as history had known it, as the furthest social experiment in the Buddha's inner revolution, was brought to an end.

The Dalai Lama was reasonably well received in India, and the rapidly growing numbers of Tibetan refugees were given roadworking jobs or land grants and were allowed to develop their own school system. His Holiness focused his efforts on building the institutions necessary to preserve the Tibetan culture in the hearts and minds of the people in exile, and on his own continuing studies and practice of Buddhist meditation. Monasteries sprang up in exile, in India and Nepal. As in Tibet, more than 10 percent of the male population enrolled for the traditional monastic education, though they modified the monastic life to include agricultural labor, since the refugee economy did not have the surplus that had been available in Tibet to support the full-time studies of the monks and nuns. The rest of the refugee community adapted to life in India, largely settling in subsistence communities on lands given to them by the government of India. The Tibetans were honored in 1995 as one of the world's model refugee communities. Two generations of Tibetans have grown up in exile retaining Tibetan literacy, the Tibetan sense of identity, and Buddhist religious beliefs, and most still hope that the world will someday honestly recognize the reality and right of their existence.

The Tibetan people and their energy are now dispersed throughout the world. Just as the momentum of the enlightenment movement was consolidated in Tibet at the end of the first millennium, so now it has been forced out into the larger world at the end of the second. The enlightenment movement has begun to spread in the West.

The politics-of-enlightenment perspective equates civilization with gentleness, and one measure of its strength in a society is where one stands on a scale from monasticism to militarism. The Europeans destroyed their monastic preserves, while they secularized and militarized their energies. Their restless internal discontent led them to expand their populations, overflow their habitats, and spill all over the entire world, creating an outer modernism whose weaknesses weigh heavily on the earth.

It is not that the centuries of Western modernization have been utterly fruitless or that it would have been better for Europe to have remained in thrall to medieval superstition and blind faith. It is essential that Europe, and all the human world, woke up from the suppressive authoritarian ideologies and discovered a natural self-confidence in the power and potential of humanity. But negative impulses almost always awaken along with the positive ones, and after throwing off the yoke of dominance, people have the task of finding methods of self-restraint. Liberation in general is an unqualified good, but once a person is freed, there are endless new problems of getting an education, unlearning negative ideas, learning self-discipline, and cultivating new abilities.

The Western and Eastern outer and inner enlightenment movements each in their own way broke through the confusions of dualism, sparking different ideas about responsibility and conscious individual autonomy.

If there is anything to the thesis that our Western modernity is not the only modernity and that the alternative, inner modernity may be not merely viable but essential and possibly even superior, then the transition to postmodernity takes on a very different aspect. When we believe our materialistic modernity is the only one, we see postmodernity as nihilistic and chaotic. Those who abhor the brutality of industrial modernity feel compelled to revert to a plethora of traditionalities, while those who find that reversion terrifying cling to an ever more technologically elaborate materialistic modernity and turn a blind eye to the destructive effects of population explosion, pollution, resource depletion, and species extinction.

It is truly a major discovery that there is an alternative modernity, an inner, spiritual, individual modernity that requires neither unrelenting materialistic industrial destruction of the planet nor a retreat into an imagined primitivistic utopia, a modernity that calls us to move forward in transforming ourselves and our world to gain a quality of life higher than any we have ever known. If there is a better, more satisfying way to be modern, we can work toward a life-saving new synthesis of outer and inner modernities. The task before us now is to deepen our interconnectedness and free ourselves thoroughly from alienation. Then our unified consciousness can only improve each individual's sense of inextricable interconnectedness with all others, and we will never be caught in the destructive rampage inevitably unleashed by any form of alienation.

The Fourteenth Dalai Lama's perspective on world events offers us a key to his optimism. He discerns four differences between the beginning and the ending of the twentieth century, which he considers the bases for hope in the twenty-first century.

His first ground for hope is the possibility of a shift from a military to a peaceful means of resolving disputes. In 1900, the power of war went practically unchallenged as the final arbiter of people's fates. Military institutions dominated the world, driving technological developments and building the largest arsenals in planetary history. Now the military approach has overwhelmed itself, its weapons have become too gigantic to use, its mode of social mobilization is bankrupt. Peace is coming to be seen as a paramount value in itself, and nonviolence on various levels is beginning to come to the fore as the more plausible method for settling social problems.

This first premise about the situation at the start of the twentieth century is unexceptional. In retrospect, everyone would agree about the social and cultural climate that led to the world wars. That peace is the conscious goal is agreeable to most, but few yet consider nonviolence powerful enough to achieve it. On the other hand, Gandhi's success with the British empire, and Nelson Mandela's success in South Africa after renouncing the violence integral to the African National Congress's original strategy, point to the viability of nonviolence. The Palestinian success in liberating some of the West Bank and Gaza just by renouncing violence, even though violent extremists from both sides are constantly jeopardizing that process; the velvet revolution in Czechoslovakia; the unification of Germany; the liberation of the Baltic States and the Ukraine; and so forth—these are emerging examples of the power of nonviolence over violence. Tibet's continuing tragedy; the intransigence of the Chinese dictatorship with regard to its own democratic movement; the persistence of the Burmese junta; the Bosnian conflict—these are counterexamples, though in each case there still is realistic hope for eventual victory of the nonviolent as the weakness of the violent oppressors becomes increasingly evident.

The Dalai Lama's second basis for hope is the individual.
In 1900, people placed their hope in social systems. They
considered government institutions and efficient bureaucratic organizations, whether capitalist or communist, to be
the key to human success, and they thought the individual
should be controlled and kept in servitude. The fascist systems brought us world war and the slaughter of more than
a hundred million people, and the great state systems based
on the dictatorship of the proletariat oppressed their citizens
in a lethal manner. As Vaclav Havel has said, the last effort of
the Western Enlightenment to engineer the perfect social
system—based on Marxist sociological principles and their
underlying Judaeo-Christian utopianism—has disastrously
and definitively failed. So the great dream of socialism—liberation by submerging the individual in the social system—
has proven a nightmare.

In the "free world," some still may think that the capitalist system has proven its effectiveness and superiority over
the failed communism. Certainly the basic idea of capitalism,
to produce more than you consume and thereby save concentrated value for others and for future generations, re-
flects detachment, self-restraint, even generosity, and
therefore has a good impulse in its core. The solid mercantile impulse is definitely one step higher as a means of livelihood than the militaristic, predatory raiding of neighbors. At
least there is a potential enrichment of each party in the exchange. One party does not kill and deprive all others of
wealth. On the other hand, capitalism exploits resources and

people. It has provided well for a minority of elites, but those people also are not free of the harmful effects of excessive greed. The people in the middle are the luckiest, suffering enough to be stimulated to creativity by healthy challenges, yet having enough leisure and respite from stress to find pleasure and face their creative challenges. But they are increasingly scared of the resentment of the poor beneath them, more and more stressed by the insatiable demands of the excessively wealthy above them. In short, the people at the top, middle, and bottom of our still-uncivilized world systems are slowly waking up to the fact that they are not that well served by it. But this situation is not irremediable.

The shift during the twentieth century that the Dalai Lama finds hopeful is not a movement from one state system to another. It is the shift of emphasis from great collectives—impersonal, faceless systems that suppress individuality—to great individuals. The purpose of human life is the evolutionary development of each human individual. Therefore the purpose of society is the education and empowerment of its individuals. Democracy is the form of social organization (or disorganization) that encourages individual empowerment most directly. Therefore, as Winston Churchill said, it is the worst form of government imaginable, except for all the others.

The last overarching system subject to this critique must be nationalism. Nationalism is a final stumbling block to true world citizenship, true world governance, to an overriding sense of self-identity of the individual as a human being, because it submerges the individual in a falsely absolute group identity that increases our separation from all those defined as "others" and sees them as potential threats. Once this shift from system to individual has taken hold more fully, people will be more resistant to ideological fanaticism and not easily mobilized into vast armies to promote any system.

The Dalai Lama's third source of hope is the shift away from the view that materialistic science and technology bring ultimate power to shape life and destiny. Early in the twentieth century, it seemed that with a few more decades of progress, the elements would come totally under human control, the mind would reveal all its secrets, and even synthetic immortality might be achieved. Now it is increasingly clear that science gains more knowledge only about how much it does not know, and that technological fixes lead to new problems.

Materialism is an ideological distortion, and people are beginning to turn to religious traditions for alternative perspectives on reality, in some cases trying to resuscitate modes of belief long discredited by science. The Tibetan tradition of spiritual science can make a key contribution. Because of its emphasis on the examination of reality, it can help bring inner and outer sciences together to achieve real benefit for individuals and also leave room for spiritual awareness.

Science, as the organized pursuit of knowledge of reality through precise observation and critical reasoning, is not the problem of materialism. The carefully inquiring mind that science nurtures was celebrated by the Buddha as the highest human enterprise long before modernity. The challenge posed by the enlightenment traditions is not a fundamentalist rejection of science or a regression to nonrational consciousness. It is rather the critique of the dogma of materialism and the resurrection of the spiritual sciences to complement the material sciences. The enlightenment movement is a discipline of inner science, an organized and systematic pursuit of the knowledge of the reality of self and environment through precise observation and critical reasoning. It posits that it is possible to achieve a complete knowledge of all reality, a knowledge that does enable perfect mastery of all conditions of life and death in order to attain perfect happiness. It further postulates that this knowledge can be taught and shared with other beings, so that eventually all will come to the full understanding of which all are capable. Therefore, the enlightenment tradition welcomes the aspiration of progress that drives materialist sciences.

The enlightenment tradition does not demand even that inquirers believe that there is such a thing as enlightenment. It urges them only to critique more carefully their metaphysical presuppositions and to augment their methods to include interior observation, using contemplative techniques to make the subjective mind itself a polished instrument of penetrating and transformative insight; to think critically;

to doubt all things under the sun and beyond the moon, within as well as without; to challenge even Descartes on the seemingly self-evident thinking self that seems indubitably to be here.

The enlightenment movement does present historical evidence about the efficacy of its methods and the desirability of its results, as witnessed in the lives of its practitioners in many cultures over millennia. And so it presents itself as an excellent stimulator of other religions to bring forward their spiritual sciences, not just in order to revive their myths but as an ideal partner for modern sciences. This new harmony between inner and outer science should be a major element of life in the twenty-first century.

The Dalai Lama's fourth ground of hope is the growing understanding that the world's ecosystem is a fragile network of living things. In 1900, the environment was seen as inert and mechanical, as raw material awaiting human manipulation and exploitation. Water, air, earth, trees, minerals, and animals—all were used up with ever-increasing efficiency. While governments and corporate institutions still are adding to the crisis by taking a short-term view of costs and benefits, the view of our human life as inexorably connected to the living web of nature is slowly prevailing, and the tide is turning toward a genuine and widespread wish to care for our common mother earth.

Much of our worst environmental destruction has come from our exaggerated sense of the sovereign, static, isolated

self. From that perspective, everything else is alien, disconnected, and so we were thrown into a state of mutually lethal
tension with them. Our much vaunted Western civilization
took a wrong turn all the way back in the Hellenic era, which
is underlined by Shantideva's famous shoe-leather analogy
for our having made control over outer nature a priority
over control of inner nature: "Who doesn't want to hurt his
feet when he walks the rough and brambly earth has two
choices; either cover the earth with leather or make himself
a pair of sandals." We in the West have been trying vainly to
make the earth into a perfect softball, sewing it up in the
leather of protective material smoothness, trying to save
human sensitivity by changing and rearranging the outer environment. The Indian and Tibetan enlightenment movement took the other turn. It decided that the "foot" of the
sensitive human mentality should learn to protect itself with
the "sandal" of self-mastery, that internal understanding and
control are more practically achievable than total control of
the infinite external.

However, India and Tibet, while they did not disregard
the external sciences, focused on sandal making to the ex-
clusion of developing control of the outer world. In Tibet,
the external sciences were neglected in recent centuries,
and the physical infrastructure became deficient. The culture
of inner modernity needs our outer sciences just as we need
its inner sciences.

These four grounds for hope—the reawakening of the

human love of peace; the esteem for individual freedom; the craving for nondual wisdom that unites the spiritual and the material; and the acceptance of ecological relationship— resonate intriguingly with four of the five principles of the politics of enlightenment: nonviolence, individualism, education, and altruistic correctedness. The fifth, global democratism, is exemplified in His Holiness the Great Fourteenth Dalai Lama himself.

We are at what some call the end of history, waiting either for oblivion or for the advent of cool heroes who can put their lives on the line for peace, as past ages' hot heroes did for glory. We have seen the progress of the enlightenment movement in India and Tibet coming down to us here and now. How can this movement assist our entire civilization to weather the crisis we face?

Clearly the Fourteenth Dalai Lama and those Tibetans who stand nonviolently with him against the oppression of China's government are just such heroes, persisting against all odds to challenge the backward-thinking leaders of the world's most populous nation. Gorbachev and those who stood with Boris Yeltsin against the coup have shown cool heroism; they have already changed the face of the earth. Lech Walesa and Vaclav Havel have led such heroes to victory. Corazón Aquino and her followers; Aung San Suu Kyi and her supporters—all of these have shown cool heroism, sometimes winning, sometimes losing, but triumphing by sticking to their vision of peace. The students of Tiananmen Square stood up with cool heroism before the whole world; they were crushed as the world looked on, and yet they continue their struggle. The Tibetans persist in their nonviolent struggle. The odds seem great against those cool heroes and heroines who still seem to be losing. Is there real hope for them?

Most of the teachers from the various enlightenment movements seem to agree on one thing: If there is to be a renaissance of enlightenment science in our times, it will have to begin in America. America is the land of extreme dichotomies: the greatest materialism and the greatest disillusionment with materialism; great self-indulgence and great self-transcendence. People in America by and large are at least half-nihilistic, cosmically fearless, believe in nothing but what they can see, despair of any sort of meaning in their existence, and are fragmented in their sense of identity. The enlightenment movement can bring a full range of identity-analysis tools as well as self-esteem-building disciplines and arts so that Americans can realize individual king- and queen-ship.

For the most part, Americans have backed away from hot heroism into cool passivity. This is a step in the right direction. We have gained sensitivity in wanting to avoid the pain and suffering attendant upon doing hot battle with external enemies, as well as the wisdom of recognizing the specious reasons for which political leaders will send their men to war. For intelligent persons, these are good grounds to refuse the trumpets of battle.

Some thinkers see a major paradigm shift under way from patriarchy not back to matriarchy, but to something new, to a true democratic equality between the sexes that can unleash their full creative powers in a shared transformation. Tibetan Buddhism may help us discover a symbol for the ultimate that goes beyond God the Father or God the Mother to God-and-Goddess as the Father-Mother union. The tantric deities are depicted in sexual union, and it is the individual's practice to be able to manifest this Father-Mother union. The enlightenment movement has fostered the individual skills that make society workable in new male-female-balanced, nonauthoritarian, democratic forms. It has developed effective systems to cultivate the tolerance that can flow with noncontrol; the openness with information; the warm interest in and the ability to associate with others; the flexibility of character coming from deep self-esteem, sensitivity, and gentleness; the lack of submissiveness to authority; and the reliance on one's own good sense and reasonable understanding.

Will there be a movement of cool heroism in America? Will we be able to produce and support such leaders here? If so, could he or she win power? What would be the campaign strategy in line with the politics of enlightenment? How do we as individuals develop cool heroism ourselves? How do we engage in the politics of enlightenment on the day-to-day level?

The politics of enlightenment since Ashoka proposes a truth-conquest of the planet—a Dharma-conquest, meaning a cultural, educational, and intellectual conquest. These are conquests in which realistic insight, liberative art, generosity, justice, tolerance, and enterprise encourage other individuals in other nations to develop these qualities in themselves and in their countries. This kind of liberating conquest is quite different from military imperialism, where we simply control others' external behaviors by force, from economic imperialism, where we use the threat of military might to force economic deals on people. It is different also from propaganda-conquest, whereby a false reality is presented to people deprived of access to full information, and an ideology is imposed on them by force.

There is much to build on in American modernity and American spirit. What is good about this American modernity? What wouldn't we ever give up? What are we willing to fight the world for? Life! What do we mean by that? We mean that one's individual life should be the primary concern of all other people, and that all other people's lives should be one's primary concern. Subsistence for everyone should be guaranteed by the whole society. No one has the right to take it away for his or her gain. No one can ask for its sacrifice for his or her own petty ends. Our individual existences are the central aim of the whole society. We each can feel that everyone else is there for us, and can develop the compassionate wisdom that we are there for everyone else.

Liberty. Freedom. What do we mean by that? We mean the individual's opportunity to choose anew, each generation, his or her vocation for life, how to spend his or her creative energies. This means educational opportunity for all classes, races, and sexes. This means health and welfare standards for all. This means legal protection for minorities, women, children, disadvantaged people of any kind. And it means a system of governance that systematically prevents one individual or group from exploiting any other individual or group.

The pursuit of real happiness. What do we mean by that? That we do not live by bread alone. That all our opportunity will be stultifying and boring if we do not know what makes us happy and how to pursue it. That happiness should be ours and that there are methods for discovering which happiness is really reliable and satisfying, and then securing that in an enduring way without depriving others.

America has the opportunity today to start the ball rolling. We are beginning to try to see reality clearly and to build on that personally and socially, in spite of our persistently misguided, backward-thinking national leadership. I take my cue from Jefferson's second inaugural, wherein he considers the planet and sees our experiment as the last best hope to move humanity beyond the groaning and the struggling within the traditional bonds of ego- and nation-identity definitions.

We have made peace more powerful than war by developing weapons whose escalation consequences go beyond imagination. War now has become a winnerless proposition for those with full information and all their marbles.

We have almost caught up with India culturally by learning the importance of exalting the individual. Though she was badly wrecked by a millennium of conquerors, India walks closely with us as the world's largest democracy today in implementing individualism on the political level.

We are beginning to respect spiritual as well as material science. We have come to realize that you need wisdom to wield knowledge. We have the Deweyan pragmatism about religious theories and disciplines, and we are putting every conceivable method recommended into experimental practice. We have from the past the knowledge of what works, and the ability to elaborate even better methodologies as we turn our ingenuity toward them.

Our tradition of open-heartedness and warm outgoingness prepares us for a healthy, universally inclusive relatedness rather than a paranoid alienation. In spite of the continuing regressive efforts by many in big business, we are among the world's leaders in environmentalism, though still we are far from winning the battle against the confused savagery of greed, aggression, and blind convictions even in our own society.

We have internalized a negative deity from ancient times—the jealous god, the wrathful god, the god of vengeance and punishment, the autocratic One who appears to need no validation, seems to stand outside of all relationship, unaccountable, thundering, "I am that I am!" This is the declaration that creates a tyrant, and it is exemplified in the many we have suffered. Hitler, Stalin, and Mao were held in power by their beliefs in their own independent existence, as well as the forms of authoritarianism current in their cultures. Our authoritarian culture still produces autocratic leaders. Our authoritarian personality structures make us afraid and unable to participate in democracy, to make it work. It makes us afraid to be kings and queens ourselves, hence we project kingly ability on others who only pretend to knowledge, compassion, and ability.

In spite of all the reasons for a positive twenty-first century, we always feel, "This can never be! It will never happen!" This feeling is itself the cause of the world's persisting in violent madness through the last hundred centuries, with only short breaks during the brief visits of buddhas. Because of this feeling we spend a major part of our life energies and our world's resources in coping, with an attitude of hopelessness, having some relative and temporary successes but remaining certain of the one truth that we'll never really succeed. We see ours as a poorly made or evolved life on an inadequate planet inhabited by dissatisfied and untrustworthy beings. We struggle on as prisoners of a history that goes from personal misery to universal doomsday.

Nothing but our own stubbornness and misplaced convictions is stopping us from turning all this around. We can know everything if only we learn to look at what we know and separate the false from the real. We have adequate ability to fix everything on the relative infrastructure level, if only we share all we know and if individuals do not harm one another in order to pursue some wrongly defined objective such as self-aggrandizement through the accumulation of unnecessary wealth. If we were to scrap the military, the combined defense budgets of the world's major powers could make a cornucopia of Africa's soil to support its people in a few years' time.

History's enlightenment movements tell us we can transform ourselves and our world. We can even train ourselves to die enjoyably. We can continue suffering the periodic hells that our ignorance produces; we can continue to listen to those who say that we'll go mad for thinking we can do anything about the world. Or we can start by allowing that it might be possible to make an enlightened society, one individual at a time, starting with the obvious: ourselves. If, once we enter into the process of enlightening ourselves, we find it possible to help other people move in the same direction, so much the better. If more people can move their minds and change their hearts, even better. If we don't see the whole move into a buddhaverse manifestation in our lifetimes, at least we will have been part of the potential solution rather than of the problem.

Our presidential system was created as a substitute for the British monarchy. George Washington chose not to be

George the First of America in order to prevent the degeneracy that results from power being vested in a dynastic family line, and in order to redistribute to free citizens the fragment of the kingly power that is the individual vote. The essential ideal of our system was for each citizen to be a king, to rule him- or herself, and to exercise responsibility for the entire common good. Tom Paine captured well this turning moment in planetary history with his wonderful image of shattering the crown of royal dominion and giving each citizen a jeweled piece. According to myth, Maitreya, the future Buddha, will shatter his inherited jeweled sacrificial post and distribute a piece to each of his thousands of disciples, all of whom will immediately attain liberation and enlightenment.

It is not an exaggeration to say that the true greatness of America has come from this ideal. In allowing each citizen to feel some spark of royal confidence and vibrant dignity and generosity, an immense creativity was unleashed in our people. There is no doubt that this creativity is what makes America loved by the people of the whole world, what makes America's lifestyle so much admired and imitated. America's misguided racism, militarism, and nondemocratic politics are the causes of all its failures and shortcomings and have damaged America's good image immeasurably. If we reawaken our positive vision and creative action, it is still not too late to restore the alignment of the democratic outer revolution with the inner revolution of enlightenment. We must reaffirm the democratic mission to restore a piece of the jewel crown of the natural royalty of every individual to every person on this planet, letting the authoritarian personalities of dictators and dictated melt in the glow of the human beauty and creativity released by freedom.

Epilogue

Working Axioms
for Realizing
and Implementing
Inner Revolution
and a Politics
of Enlightenment

1. Life is boundless; it has an infinite horizon of positive development as well as an infinite danger of degeneration. There is an ultimate goal for human evolution, an enlightened state, a full development of wisdom, love, happiness, and power that is beyond even our wildest dreams, inconceivable to our habitual notions.

2. Materialists and nihilists have no room for such an ideal and so close off the possibility for themselves. Theistic mystics have identified such a life as the life of God and as possible for rarely blessed humans only through union with God. But Buddhists have identified such a state as that of an enlightened person, a perfect buddha. They consider it accessible to everyone, for anyone can and everyone will become enlightened buddhas themselves.

3. The perfect enlightenment of buddhahood—selfless freedom—transcends all dichotomies and is just as power-

ful in the social realm as it is peaceful in personal experience. Its core insight is the full embrace of the inexorable relatedness of the selfless individual to all others. Nagarjuna expressed such enlightened reality as "having the essence of emptiness and compassion."

4. Buddhahood as universal love and wisdom is the supreme power, the diamond vajra strong force that blazes from every atom of every universe. Buddhahood manifests itself actively in human society as an inner revolution, a politics of enlightenment.

5. Since a "world" is more accurately a collective mind-field of living beings than a mass of inorganic elements, to become a buddha means to transform the entire mind-field, to become a mythical world-conqueror. Doing so is considered to have a far greater effect on the world than conquering the whole world physically.

6. Buddhahood is the complete truth-conquest of the whole world, the creation of a perfect buddha-environment, although the unfolding of this buddhaverse appears to take time from the perspective of the unenlightened people trapped in ordinary time or history.

7. A buddha's enlightenment is expressed as the ultimate artistry of planet-transformation. This art unfolds gradually through history as the process of taming violence by nonviolence, what we all know as "progress" or the "advance of civilization."

8. Buddhaverse development is especially appropriate for human beings, in that the human species is most close to

buddhahood. The human life-form is itself a very high embodiment of evolutionary generosity, sensitivity, and tolerance, developed over long eons of individual evolutionary
struggle.

9. Truth-conquest, or buddhaland building, can proceed
only nonviolently, since individuals can be conquered only
from the inside, from their hearts, by their own free understanding. Their transformative insight itself is what liberates
the energy of the general goodwill that constitutes the perfected land.

10. Hence perfect buddhas must carry on their truth-
conquest by means of education in the liberative sense, which
is neither indoctrination nor training.

11. The insight of psychological selflessness has been the
inexhaustible source of the creative individualism that Buddhism has always nurtured. It has been also the liberator of
the world-transforming dynamism of the ethical selflessness
that shines through the history of the Buddhist societies. An
inner revolution's politics of enlightenment is designed to
allow individuals in societies to develop in an optimal way.

12. The educational institution Shakyamuni Buddha
founded is the Jewel Community (Samgharatna). It is an alternative social world founded on enlightenment, detachment, and love (the ordinary social world is founded on
delusion, greed, and anger). It functions on the moral, spiritual, and intellectual levels as the matrix of the new ethics,
new religions, and new sciences.

13. Monasticism is the core of the Jewel Community. It is

an original invention of the Buddha. It spurs society to acknowledge that its highest collective interest is none other than the self-fulfillment of its individuals. The enlightened individual's deliberate persistence in the total renunciation of the ordinary social world is itself the most radical and powerful of all political acts, grounding the politics of enlightenment solidly on the preeminence of the transcendent.

14. The monastic core provides the cocoon for the free creativity of the lay Jewel Community, which needs special assistance to maintain its enlightenment principles in confrontation with the militaristic harshness of the ordinary social world.

15. Monasticism is a mediating institution, centrist in every sense, midway between city and wilderness, priest and hermit, noble and commoner, indirectly providing both social cohesion and mobility. It is the shelter and training ground for the nonviolent "army," the shock troops for the sustained social revolution the Buddha initiated in order to transform societies based on ignorance and selfishness into societies based on wisdom and enlightenment.

16. The main rival of monasticism is imperialistic militarism, the core institution for secular and religious rulers of ordinary societies. Militarism is anchored in organizations in which the human being's basic feeling of enlightenment is trained out and armored over, encouraging individual regression to subhuman insensitivity, viciousness, and harmfulness. Militarism allows for a politics of compulsion, if it allows for any politics at all.

17. Since the Buddha's time, the monastic-based Jewel Community has gradually gained ground over militaristic societies by promoting a sensibility of humaneness, laying the foundation for the politics of enlightenment.

18. This politics of enlightenment is based on transcendental individualism, heroic pacifism, educational universalism, social altruism, and democratic liberalism.

19. This politics of enlightenment, as a body of theory and repertoire of practical strategies, has always lain and still does lie at the hearts of the more durable and effective social and political systems in all parts of the planet in all eras of history. In fact, the very idea and the practical art of politics flow from enlightenment achieved by humans in the effort to open the creative social space for individual growth and communal enjoyment; politics itself is a middle way between the two extreme states of ordinary societies, the states of battle and ritual.

20. The politics of enlightenment continues to defeat the politics of compulsion (as proven by our continued survival) because of not only the moral force of its principles but also its natural alliance with the mercantile expansion of wealth and the bureaucratic maintenance of popular governments.

21. The Jewel Community operates on three levels in every culture in which it exerts its influence: revolutionary, evolutionary, and fruitional or millennial.

22. The revolutionary phase is radically dualistic. During it, the Jewel Community presents itself as an alternative to ordinary society, stresses its own religious distinctiveness,

and disclaims any attempt to actively intervene in the society's affairs.

23. The evolutionary phase is *educatively* nondualistic. The Jewel Community asserts its own power in the society by promoting a new social ethic through a variety of lay educational institutions that surround the monastic core.

24. The millennial phase is *pervasively* nondualistic. During it, the society is able to enjoy the universe of enlightenment, and Jewel Community institutions openly take responsibility for the society's direction. This last phase is most exceptional in history, still mainly a potentiality for the future.

25. Tibetan society is the only one in planetary history in which this third phase has been partially reached.

26. Elements of the fruitional phase were central in the Renaissance and Reformation that eventually created the modern world, but materialistic extremism twisted the Western transformation into the mirror opposite of the fruitional.

27. The modern world—with its secular nondualism ineffectively restrained by an array of transcendentalist absolutisms—has come to the brink of the abyss of total self-annihilation.

28. Therefore, now, today, it is obvious that the implementation of the politics of enlightenment is the only way to avoid planetary disaster.

29. All one needs to understand the inner revolution and live the politics of enlightenment is wisdom about one's

long-term self-interest, good-humored tolerance of one's own and others' faults, trust in the adequacy of the environment and our fellow beings, and the courage to take up the responsibility of enlightenment.

30. Buddha is as buddha does. Just be happy. At least act enlightened. Feel enlightened. It is more pleasant, and enlightenment itself will follow.

Some Contemporary Ideas for an Actual Political Platform Based on Enlightenment Principles

*T*his platform does not pretend to be anything more than a challenge to existing parties in functioning democracies anywhere in the world, an archetypal set of planks that are meant to stimulate discussion in an actual political process. It is based on the five principles of the politics of enlightenment: transcendent individualism, nonviolent pacifism, educational evolutionism, ecosocial altruism, and universal democratism. It applies them to the more difficult issues of our current world politics and spurs a process of thinking about a modern enlightenment politics. I offer this platform in the spirit of the inner revolution, to enlist others in the creation of a vision of enlightenment potential becoming mainstream in the world today.

Planks from this platform can be adopted by the existing parties into their own platforms. It is not necessary for us to wait for the founding of a new party to try to implement the enlightenment principles, though such a new party may indeed become necessary and practical in one country or another, one day or another. It is never too soon to begin to think about how principles can be put into practice. The inner revolution is not just something that happened long ago and far away. It is going on today within the hearts and minds of billions of people. Already it has emerged naturally within the principles, if not always the practices, of our modern democracies. The time is always good for the inner revolution to take practical effect on actual policies and practices to change all our lives for the better.

With an enlightenment-oriented platform, candidates could reinspire electorates with new visions of their countries and the world as a whole. Harping on the "enlightenment" underpinning of these planks is not even necessary, but candidates should argue their rational, spiritual, humanistic, and scientific bases. We do not need to hide the platform's enlightened, idealistic bent.

In this new, modern, political life, we would learn how to get back to our basic democratic ideals; take back our destiny from faceless, impersonal systems; and lead the world of billions of individual people into a new age. Its practicality is self-evident. The mongers of defeatism and apathy would be exposed as the cynical tyrants that they are, selling our planet down the river—selling it much too cheaply.

Organized opposition from entrenched power groups, using all sorts of unethical tactics to prevent people from

thinking about what is really in everyone's best interests, poses a great danger to such platforms. Therefore,
enlightenment-oriented candidates must be well researched,
well managed, well communicated, and well guarded. The
great advantage of such platforms is that they can be sold easily to the general public and the world public, since they
offer sensible and practical solutions to problems that have
been created and maintained for quite a while now by short-
term selfishness on the part of the few and by long-
entrenched, blind inertia of habit on the part of the many.

One of the keys to an enlightenment-inspired platform is
that the practical problems of world management are not
that hard to solve. People should be persuaded that things are
workable and that enlightened leadership can make the difference. People's optimism and determination must be mobilized by a clear and holistic assessment of the situation.
Defeatism, apathy, cynicism, despair—these are invoked by
the few who do better when the world is managed badly,
when the many are prevented from demanding and implementing good management.

Here are ten suggested platform planks, with some explanation of each. They are intentionally somewhat general,
since the details can be developed only by the group process
in party conventions, wherein actual applications of the principles can be worked out. Though these platforms can be
adopted in democracies as varied as the United States, Ar-
gentina, India, South Africa, Sweden, or Russia, my thinking

departs naturally from the realities of U.S. society today, which, in some sense, bad as well as good, has taken the trends of modern industrial democracy to their furthest experimental levels politically, socially, and culturally.

FIRST: We affirm the priority of the individual over the community in all areas. Thus, we support all individual-oriented policies. We proclaim the modern democratic system the most individualistic form of government in history and therefore the most successful. We fully admit to its imperfect and unfinished nature, and heartily invite all peoples, either those oppressed within or excluded without, to join it in creating a truly democratic, spiritually individualistic United Nations of Earth.

It is a fact that the first meaning of Siddhartha's renunciation, affirmed by Shakyamuni again and again after enlightenment, is that the individual has the highest duty of him- or herself: to evolve from an egocentric being into an enlightened one. Societies' highest interests lie in supporting individuals' attempts to do so. The Jewel Community was founded on these principles 2,500 years ago, and they are the heart of modern democracy. Jefferson and company followed in the English civil-liberty tradition and also absorbed the influence of the Native American societies, which were far more individualistic and less hierarchical than the European ones and which allowed individuals a much higher degree of personal power. Thus, the colonists eventually felt the yoke of the British imperial mentality to be intolerable and sought to throw it off. They enshrined this feeling of wanting to be themselves, wanting more freedom from authoritarian tradition, in the Declaration of Independence, the Bill of Rights, and in the system of conferring authority on rulers by individual and periodic vote.

Lately this democratic process has been effectively threatened by virtual autocrats who have pretended to champion the individual and his or her liberty against the supposedly oppressive domination by "big government." These corporate spokepersons have used the "big lie" technique and have come close to subverting democracy in the name of individual liberty. They have led revolts to diminish taxes for the very rich; called for law and order to imprison the very poor; tried to reestablish racist dominance patterns; attacked women's rights to choose their roles and relations; pretended to defend religious freedom to promote religious bigotry; supported a demented international arms industry and an insane level of citizenry armament; attempted to remove all protections of the environment from short-sighted exploitation; and generally fostered a sense of alienation, apathy, and confusion among the people. It is therefore essential that we reassume the idealistic high ground of democratic political activism and put libertarian principles at the fore of all policies. A skillful arguing of these principles will solve the major tough issues of the day and reinvite the divisive, single-issue splinter groups into a winning coalition. To succeed, we must try to present enlightenment reinforcement as a developing middle way through the crippling polarizations.

Under this first, most fundamental plank, we must restore to people the pride they once took and can again discover in self-transcendence, in heroic struggle for a positive ideal, in liberty invested in opening the millennium to all. We can restore pride in democracy internationally by showing leadership in liberty, not in military adventures, not in neoimperialistic support of rapacious corporations, not in nuclear terrorism but by setting the example in idealism, in peacefulness, in pluralism, in generosity, in responsibility. Since the end of the Cold War, the world has needed, more than anything, a vibrant, multinational Peace Corps—the export of a democratic way of cheerful liberty; disciplined civility; and innovative creativity, altruism, and heroism. In fighting off totalitarianism, we have become too much like our enemies, infected with their habits (some of our leaders even prefer the friendly foreign dictator to the obstreperous foreign democrat). We must be uncompromising in our dealings with the remaining dictatorships, especially those in China, Burma, Indonesia, North Korea, Vietnam, Iraq, Sudan, and anywhere else they may reemerge.

Democracy's quintessential universalism must be re-evoked as an ideal goal for the entire planet. It must be rechanneled away from the militarism inherited from World War II and the Cold War and turned into an Ashokan-Gandhian–style peace-conquest or truth-conquest of the world. America's experience with, and still-possible success at, the pluralistic lifestyle should be a beacon for the world. We should not give up too quickly the effort to form a freedom police force for the world and should show how it will gradually and systematically continue to turn its powers over to the global community of the United Nations of Earth. In addition, the citizens of free countries in all parts of the world should serve as artists and visionaries to all the peoples, exporting jazz and rock, film and fashions, computers and solar cells.

S E C O N D : Acknowledging the very grave injustices that are still inflicted on billions of beings, we proclaim everyone's right to equality of opportunity in all respects, regardless of racial, sexual, religious, national, ethnic, or economic group membership, and we deny any group's right to oppress its individuals under the cloak of national sovereignty, religious absolutism, or any other excuse.

The quota issue and affirmative action policies have been the targets of racist backlash and have been exploited by special-interest politicians trying to present themselves as libertarians, especially those solicitous for white liberties. We should take this mask of so-called libertarianism away from such politicians and show how the inclusion of the disenfranchised enriches all others, how the adoption of militaristic, fascistic oppression policies is just an excuse for paranoid elites to oppress us all. We should adopt Malcolm X's brilliant idea and allocate a hundred dollars a head for every minority member and also create large lobbying foundations in Washington, a $3.5 billion African-American Foundation, a $1.5 billion Asian-American Foundation, a $1 billion Native American Foundation, and so forth. Indian affairs should be moved out of the Department of the Interior into its own special agency, perhaps as part of a minority superagency. We should affirm vigorously Jefferson's vision of pluralistic equality and expose racist backlash for the self-destructive piece of denial that it is. These policies in America should become the basis of a new level of self-determination in the numerous countries worldwide that are torn apart by majority/minority oppression. In the twentieth century, more people were killed by their own governments than by enemies in wars, and there cannot be world democracy until all peoples feel truly represented by their national governments.

THIRD: We pledge to adopt a fully consensual tax system that will allow individual taxpayers to earmark their contributions for programs they choose, though for practical reasons they must give government several options.

Tax systems have led to revolts and broadscale voter disaffection, crippling governments and pushing them into deficit spending, costing everyone much because of the deteriorating quality of life, while lining the pockets of the rich and their corporations by excusing them from their share of support of the common weal. In the consensual tax system, people would be asked how they want their money spent: for schools, defense, infrastructure, welfare, research, the political system, or wherever it is needed. A computerized budgeting system could aggregate these preference figures, allowing as much money as possible to be allocated as per requests. People would be informed as to whether their money has been used as per first choice, second choice, and so on.

We should increase the graduated income tax. The government should express its partnership with corporations by helping them stay competitive in the international climate but should insist on their payment of reasonable taxes and stop them from ingenious lobbying for hidden subsidies and exemptions. Corporations should be forced to take responsibility for long-term consequences of their decisions, such as the impact on the environment, on the health of workers and customers, on the quality of life, and so on. The media, including the Internet, should be used to make all these financial operations transparent, restoring people's sense of voluntarism, participation, and responsibility, as well as government's accountability.

FOURTH: We deplore capital punishment and resolve to eradicate it in our aspiring-to-be-civilized society. We deplore also lifetime incarceration if it does not at the same time offer a full-scale evolutionary-transformation program of education. Prisons should be the education system's last line of defense and thus fully interconnected with that system's resources.

Currently, law-and-order toughness is symbolized in many countries by a willingness to execute criminals. This practice should be stopped right away. We should show an individual's rights to life, liberty, and the pursuit of happiness being upheld by society's self-restraint in situations where it could allow itself "righteous" killing. Our refusal to kill the death-row inmate should be a symbol of our strength, our ability to forego scapegoating, to look at problems more comprehensively and perceive the roots of violence within society—in bad economic patterns, bad family mores, bad education, excessive armaments, bad examples of violence in the media, and so on. As we rehabilitate ex-murderers, we rehabilitate ourselves, our society. On the other hand, we should recognize the impossibility of resolving certain situations, should not force those who crave execution to live against their will, and should acknowledge the limitedness of resources for rehabilitation in certain cases, disallowing ourselves too much righteousness in our stance.

FIFTH: We affirm each woman's right to choose for herself whether she will offer residence in her body to a new life, and therefore we pledge to deploy all forms of sex education and contraception to give women maximum control. Although we legalize abortion and make it available, aware of its serious moral, physical, and psychological consequences, we commit to supporting all possible alternatives at every phase of pregnancy, offering first-rate adoption procedures and so forth, working with the "pro-life" institutions and individuals to create ways of altering the outcomes in cases of unwanted pregnancies. Likewise, we fully support hospice care and every individual at every stage in the process of dying, and also affirm the right of terminally ill individuals to choose their own times and ways of dying.

Secular humanism's position on the abortion issue is that an individual woman has the right to choose what is going to happen in her body. Her right to life undoubtedly takes precedence over an unborn's right to life. The enlightenment politician must encourage the right-to-choose stance. However, because any loss of human life is to be greatly regretted, we must offer every facility and advantage to any woman who chooses to bring her baby to term, whether or not she is ready and/or able to keep it—great honor and respect, excellent health care, good adoption programs, a surrogate fee, and whatever we can think of and afford, inspired by our common treasuring of that potential life. If, however, the mother chooses not to have the baby, she should be given every means to safely terminate the pregnancy without incurring any stigma.

If the pro-life institutions and individuals are so outraged by the loss of life of the unborn, how can they justify holding back on sex-education and contraception programs? How can they justify not informing the young of all the realities of sexuality?

SIXTH: We affirm each individual's right to freedom of choice of lifestyles and medical therapies, free conscience in matters of religion, freedom of speech, and freedom in sexual preference—as long as these freedoms are not harmful to others. While it is a government's responsibility to protect unwary people from substances that may be harmful to them or cause them to become harmful to others, considering the disastrous failure of all efforts at prohibition of alcohol and other substances and acknowledging the fact that the wars on this or that have only enriched the criminal elements, we consider it essential that the government redirects its protective instincts toward medical, educational, and spiritual channels to cope with the habits of individuals.

The war on drugs should be acknowledged to be the failure that it is. Although billions have been expended, the drug problem is worse than ever. We must reinvoke the principle that people should be allowed to do what they want with their own bodies as long as they do not hurt others. Let us stop the government's futile attempts to regulate substance consumption and confront the ineffectiveness of all crusades of prohibition. We must terminate the incentive for criminals to smuggle drugs, regulate and tax the industries revolving around addictions, and invest the otherwise misspent billions in education and therapy. We should point out the effectiveness of the health campaign against smoking cigarettes, whereby the number of users has been diminished by tens of millions. We should educate against and deglamorize all drug use and at the same time open up the health-care industry by offering responsible alternative health-care systems true equality, thus enhancing individuals' freedom of choice.

SEVENTH: Aware of our complicity in a catastrophic misdirection of efforts and resources over this last century of militarism, we pledge to cut our defense budgets by two-thirds, reappropriating $200 billion a year in America alone and hundreds of billions in many other countries; and to build enlightened, disarmed democracies on the Tibetan and

Costa Rican models, which can lead the world toward enlightenment, liberty, and peace.

Presently, our nations and economies are paralyzed by bloated defense industries. We are bankrupted by their budgets. Militarism corrupts our quintessential liberty-oriented lifestyle. Talk of peace dividends and modest cutting cannot save the situation. We must redefine strength as the successful adaptation to peace and the progress of spreading prosperity and democracy to forestall conditions developing in other parts of the world in which the cancers of militarism and dictatorship might grow.

Our plan to redirect defense budgets should be set forth in ways everyone can understand. 1. We should show (a) how our deterrent capacity will remain in place until there is no danger of a nuclear dictatorship rising to threaten all life; (b) how pragmatism would allow us to combine our intelligence traditions with Ninja-master individual prowess and technique in order to develop a new kind of high-quality special force capable of preventing Kuwait- or Sarajevo-type scenarios; and (c) that a credible military Operation Rearguard would be maintained against any realistic threat. 2. We must prove how wasteful and counterproductive defense-industry boondoggles are. The many billions of dollars invested in fantasy-weapons programs should be recovered and put into infrastructure and cleanup programs. The space-industry firms should be assisted in turning their technology, expertise, and equipment toward peaceful uses, toward creating peace- and prosperity-enhancing goods and services. 3. We must redefine the roles of our military bases. Foreign bases might be retooled as centers for Peace Corps– or engineering corps–type development and environmental cleanup campaigns. Local bases should not be closed but rather turned into internal Peace Corps centers.

EIGHTH: We pledge to make lifelong education for all citizens the nation's top priority. We will turn prisons into real rehabilitation centers, develop well-financed educational television networks, and orient early education for all races, sexes, and classes to prepare the young to make full use of their precious human lives.

Jefferson's dream of a universal education system for all must be revived. Our platform must affirm that the highest calling of an individual is to improve him- or herself through education at whatever level. Students must be reminded constantly that their studies are the primary, foundational service of national and global interests. Adults must be encouraged to reenter education and upgrade their skills and knowledge. Academics must be rehonored, better supported, and the profession must be made more attractive to the most talented. The vast discrepancy between salary levels of doctors, lawyers, and businesspersons on the upside and teachers and professors on the downside must be rebalanced. There should be massive investment in new grade schools, complete with kindergartens and good day-care centers. Salaries of grade-school teachers should be strongly upgraded. Security, schooling, respect, dignity, honor, and esteem should be heaped upon teachers of the very young. Teen mothers and fathers especially should be supported. The racial compositions of neighborhoods would be irrelevant, for federal agencies would balance local entrenched discriminations. In fact, the most lavish expenditures should be made in the poorest neighborhoods. Schools in the ghettos should be promoted as the gateways to new lifestyles. (Of course, with the retooling of the military into largely a Peace Corps for internal infrastructure development, the ghettos would become swiftly and drastically revamped, physically, socially, artistically, morally.) High schools should receive similar upgraded levels of support and appreciation. More smaller schools should be built, with better teacher-student ratios. Ph.D.s should be mobilized and compensated to teach high school. Everyone with ability should be supported to study beyond high school. Grants, research money, scholarships, and new facilities should be broadly provided to benefit the greater number of people energized by a feeling of global renaissance.

The enlightenment traditions, free of any religious labels, could make special contributions to this educational endeavor by encouraging mind-training workshops at all levels, which would include positive-reinforcement techniques, meditation instruction, martial arts disciplines, and so forth.

At least $50 billion yearly from the defense budget savings should be set aside for such education programs at all levels. In the United States, we have been hearing from a succession of presidents how much they value education, but all they have done is cripple education. Our platform must be to restore education to its central role as the guarantor of democracy, the means to richer individual living, the central institution for the efficacious "pursuit of happiness" Jefferson mentioned.

NINTH: We reaffirm the enlightenment principle of altruistic support for all, implementing rights to a job, education, shelter, sustenance, a healthy environment, and a universal health-care system along Canadian or European lines, which would encompass a competitive plurality of health systems, including Chinese, Tibetan, Indian, and others.

The leaders of the 1980s rolled back the American and European welfare state by rejecting government's role in managing society, holding up the white racist's specter of the black welfare mother with nine children on the dole who rides in Cadillacs and swims in luxuries and so on. But this image was only a racist fantasy, and, on top of the injustice, these leaders didn't save any money at all but ran up the biggest deficits in history. What was saved in school lunches, nutrition for pregnant mothers, and so on was spent tenfold in crime prevention, prisons, and futile measures against the sheer destruction that always results from injustice. Job training was cut so that more money could be spent on unemployment benefits. Taxes were somewhat cut, but mostly for the rich, and the massive transfer of wealth to the top one percent of the population resulted not in a bonanza of investment and job creation but in a massive flight of capital to tax-sheltered investment in cheap-labor areas, with a disastrous loss of jobs and infrastructure in the developed societies. Our platform must be to reaffirm the altruistic welfare state, to prove that money invested in the lower end of the economic scale is money well spent. The removal of a poverty-ridden disaster area of the country is not only just but also saves funds in the long run and creates an incalculable treasure of human potential.

Our health platform builds on the development of universal health-care legislation that is always blocked in the United States by special interests, especially the doctors' associations and the drug, hospital, and insurance companies. The Canadian system and some of the European systems provide obvious alternatives. Enlightenment medical traditions teach the need for medicine to be universally available, thus enabling humans to stay clear of health obstructions in their efforts to utilize their human lives to evolve toward enlightenment. The industrialized medical profession has become overly mysticized but can be cured through the development of high school and undergraduate medical courses for laypersons so that the underlying science—and its glaring limitations—can be better understood. There should be many more doctors, which there could be if the physicians' guild did not enforce scarcity to insure high earnings. The insurance industries also should be brought under control, and government should work with them to create a more rational system. The drug companies should be encouraged to price more responsibly, to look for longer-term profitability and reliability. Finally, preventive medicine, diet, physical regime, exercise and fitness programs, and alternative health sciences should be encouraged, to create competitiveness for technological medicine and to give the individual more freedom of choice. The great epidemics such as heart disease, cancer, arthritis, AIDS, and stress-related disorders should be approached epidemiologically as well as individually. Fertilizer, insecticide, and food-producing and processing industries should be investigated and better restrained. Thus, the medical industries would be able once again to focus more on the common good.

TENTH: At the heart of our system, and in this hour of its crisis, we affirm the need for strong executive leadership in all democracies, reinvoking the democratic ideal that free individuals elect for their protection a strong, dedicated, trusted, and empowered chief executive. To insure that, we pledge to (1) register everyone to vote, using the computer system from the Department of Motor Vehicles; (2) use television and the telephone to create an electronic referenda system of individual feedback to the executive and legislative branches; (3) reimplement a democratic media policy to prevent monopolies over the press; and (4) finance campaigns with public money to prevent executive indebtedness to rich individuals and institutions.

The founders of the democratic society believed in the inescapable necessity for an individual to assume the burden of governance for a period of time and, further, that there were many people who could be temporarily ennobled and entrusted with that power and responsibility. We must remember that individuals throughout the land will find less support from the competing regional authorities and corporate substitutes for robber barons than they will from their entrusted central executive. In another Buddhist myth, ancient people chose Maha Sammata, the "Great Elected One," to protect themselves from potentially oppressive local competitors. Likewise, our platform should uphold an individual we can entrust—and we believe there are such individuals still out there. In the process, the system of connecting the nation's individuals with their chosen ones would be strengthened.

In addition, we should pledge to make an all-out effort to get everyone involved in the political process, to get democracy working again, and also to link individual citizens with the central executive, to make their wishes heard at a greater rate of frequency than in the occasional election. So rarely are individuals motivated to communicate with politicians that when a congressperson gets a letter, he or she considers it to represent the unarticulated thoughts of 17,000 people. Imagine how much more attentive the elected representative would be if issues were formulated on voter-referendum screens accompanying the evening news, wherein at the push of a button, an individual could register an opinion on the representative's computer! The technology is there. We should pledge to put it to use for the public benefit and not leave it for advertising companies and corporations' market research to exploit.

The majority of educated and uneducated people have become disillusioned with politicians and suspicious of all people who have wealth or influence. The incredibly selfish and self-destructive behavior of the wealthiest in the past decades has inflamed these feelings to dangerous levels. Our platform must contain a promise to reconnect the rich and powerful with the nation. The worldwide great shift of wealth and power to the top stratum of individuals has been immensely destructive to the delicate weave of most industrial societies. The fake politicians always show themselves in front of slamming jail doors, throwing switches on electric chairs, building lots of cells, and arming cops with automatic weapons—all measures taken against the already poor and oppressed. Our platform must show a real commitment to justice for all.

Enlightened activists are pro-wealth. They consider it the karmic evolutionary fruit of generosity in previous lives. A bodhisattva or messianic person wants to accumulate wealth so he or she can give it away to needy people, most creatively by investing intelligently in things that will provide long-term happiness to the people. But if wealth becomes an object of obsession, if it is used carelessly, it can be incredibly destructive, most of all to the wealthy people themselves. The enlightened democratic system institutionalizes revolution and uses progressive income taxes and other mechanisms to rebalance the rich/poor equation gently and continuously. Our platform reaffirms this policy of continuous, peaceful revolution out of compassion for both the poor and the rich. True wealth is a rich network of loving people, a pleasant and healthy lifestyle, a beautiful environment, and an inviting setting for expressing creativity. Money alone is a heavy burden, isolating its owner from real affection, ennobling unhealthy addictions, harming the environment, and causing boredom, frustration, and anxiety. Enlightenment cures all these problems through its prime virtue: generosity in all things.